The
NEPAL
COOK
BOOK

VIKING

USA | Canada | UK | Ireland | Australia
New Zealand | India | South Africa | China | Singapore

Viking is part of the Penguin Random House group of companies
whose addresses can be found at global.penguinrandomhouse.com

Published by Penguin Random House India Pvt. Ltd
4th Floor, Capital Tower 1, MG Road,
Gurugram 122 002, Haryana, India

First published in Viking by Penguin Random House India 2024

Copyright © Rohini Rana 2024

All photographs by Mannsi Agrawal, except:
Maharaja Raghvendra Dev (Introduction, p. 2)
Bikram Rai (Thakuri, Bahun, Chetri, Khas, p. 52)
Image Ark (Magar, p. 113), (Tharu, p. 180, 181, 192), (Madesh, p. 196)
Sangita Thapa (Personal Collection/Artist: Poonam Jha) (Mithila, p. 218)
Unsplash-Sudip Shrestha (Gurung, p. 121), Diya Pokharel (Mithila, p. 219)

10 9 8 7 6 5 4 3 2 1

ISBN 9780670099573

For sale in the Indian subcontinent only

Cover, illustration and design by Image Ark
Typeset in Dozza by Image Ark
Printed at Thomson Press India Ltd, New Delhi

www.penguin.co.in

The NEPAL COOK BOOK

108 REGIONAL RECIPES

ROHINI RANA

PENGUIN

VIKING

An imprint of Penguin Random House

I dedicate this book to

my family

To my beloved husband
Gen. Gaurav Shumsher Jung Bahadur Rana (retired)
Former Chief of Army Staff, Nepal Army,
for consistently savouring my cooking, encouraging me to experiment with my
culinary skills and inspiring me to write this book for future generations.

To my wonderful daughters and sons-in-law,
Malika Rajya Laxmi Pande and Sabra Bahadur Pande,
Meghna Rajya Laxmi Singh Deo and Kalikesh Narayan Singh Deo,
for always being there for me and supporting me wholeheartedly in
all my endeavours.

To my precious grandchildren,
Jaivir Bahadur Pande and Animaya Narayan Singh Deo,
Samara Bhairavi Pande and Amaira Singh Deo,
for giving me the ultimate pleasure in life and relishing my cooking.

Your unwavering love, support and appreciation are the pillars of my culinary
journey and the creation of this book. I am filled with immeasurable gratitude
for the gift of having you in my life.

AN INVITATION TO TASTE THE FLAVOURS OF NEPAL WITH A FEW OF ITS CELEBRATED PERSONALITIES

MRS ANURADHA KOIRALA

A famous social activist who manages an NGO, 'Maiti Nepal', dedicated to helping victims of sex trafficking, she has rescued and relocated over 50,000 Nepalese girls from Indian brothels. She is the winner of the 'Courage of the Conscience Award' and CNN Hero of the Year 2010. She has been awarded the Gorkha Dakshin Bahu and Tri Shakti Patta in Nepal and the Padma Shri in India, among many other honours.

Mrs Anuradha Koirala hails from a Gurung family from Rumjhatar and grew up in a large extended family. Her father was a colonel in the Indian Army in the Gorkha regiment. She has beautiful memories of a long kitchen with a firewood stove. One goat would suffice for only one and a half days to feed the large extended family members; *sukuti* (dried mutton) was their favourite food. She remembers meals cooked with *kaalo daal bhaat* (lentils and rice), with *rayo saag* (mustard greens) and *akhabari khursani hale ko golbheda achar* (tomato pickle with cherry chilli peppers). Her favourite food is daal bhaat and mustard fish curry. Golden Pekoe black leaf tea brings her maximum comfort after a hard day of work.

MRS AMBICA SHRESTHA

Mrs Ambica Shrestha is one of the first women entrepreneurs, heritage conservationists and social workers promoting the hospitality industry in Nepal. She is the president of Dwarika's Hotels and Resorts, putting Nepal on the global map. She is also the Honorary Consul for Spain, head of the Nepal Heritage Society and the head of Business and Professional Women Nepal. She was awarded The Cross of The Order of Civil Merit by HM King Juan Carlos I of Spain and Gorkha Dakshin Bahu 4th by HM King Birendra Bir Bikram Shah Dev of Nepal among other awards.

Mrs Ambica Shrestha hails from a Nepali Pradhan family in Darjeeling and is married to Dwarika Das Shrestha. He was interested in preserving the wooden artefacts and architecture in his hotel in Kathmandu; even after his death, she has continued his good work, taking the hotel to great heights.

Mrs Ambica Shrestha's favourite food is *kwati momo;* she has memories of fighting with her siblings for the delicious *momos* in the *kwati jhol. Phokso tare ko* (fried lungs) is another favourite, as well as the spicy *sande ko adua* and *bhatmas* (tempered ginger and black soya bean) from the *samay baji*. Her comfort drink is Darjeeling black tea, which takes her back to her birthplace in the hills.

MRS PUSHPA BASNET

She is the winner of the CNN Award 2012, CNN Super Hero Award 2016 and the ILGA Award from Korea.

A young social worker, founder and president of Early Childhood Development Center (ECDC) and Butterfly Home, both NGOs in Kathmandu, she works with children living with their incarcerated parents and juvenile homes, educating and rehabilitating youngsters. She has concentrated on the girl child and works tirelessly with eight government-run prisons.

Her favourite Nepali food is *daal bhaat*, to the extent that she carries her Nepali *achar* on her journeys abroad. Not much of a non-vegetarian, she enjoys the gravies more than the meat and loves raw mustard oil with her rice! She has simple eating habits and is not very adventurous with unfamiliar food.

Her favourite regional cuisine is Newari food, mainly *cheura* with meat, vegetables and tomato *bhyatal* curry. Her favourite Indian dishes are *naan* and chicken *tikka*, while her comfort food is Sherpa *kur* and *jhol tarkari*.

Her complaint with the new restaurants in Kathmandu is that food is never as good as it looks on social media advertisements. The regional cuisine is not very genuine, and she suggests the use of open kitchens so one can maintain hygiene.

About the Author

Born in Agra, she is the youngest daughter of Raja Saheb Digvijay Pal Singh and Rani Saheba Anant Kumari of Awagarh and has survived all these years with the nickname Dolly instead of Rohini! Her childhood was nothing short of idyllic, filled with love and pampering. Escaping the heat of the Indian plains, the family spent the summers in the picturesque hill station of Nainital enjoying picnics, horse riding, sailing, and the inevitable round of meticulously arranged parties to entertain summer guests. During the colder months of winter, they retreated to the tranquil, indolent ambience of Awagarh. She completed her school education at St Mary's Convent, Nainital, and graduated with a BA Honours in English Literature from Sophia College in Ajmer. Both institutions were run by nuns, which resonated with her mother, who favoured an education marked by discipline and strong moral values.

On 1 June 1960, in a visionary move for the Indian aristocracy of that time, her parents converted their summer palace into a twenty-room hotel. It is in this atmosphere of refined hospitality that she developed a deep appreciation for gourmet cuisine.

She was engaged two days before her last BA exam, having spent most of her life in a boarding school. Her mother was struck with horror as she realized her daughter had no homemaking skills, especially in cooking! Her sister-in-law, Rani Anjali Kumari, was put to the task of introducing her to the world of gastronomy. Setting aside the fictional world of Byron and Keats, Rohini began her journey of culinary discovery, and from that moment, there has been no looking back. To this very day, she has followed the passion closest to her heart.

She was married to Lt Gaurav S.J.B. Rana on 12 December 1977, who later went on to become the Chief of Army Staff, Nepal Army (2012–2015). He is the scion of seven generations in the military and the great-grandson of Maharaja Chandra S.J.B. Rana, who was the Prime Minister of Nepal for twenty-nine years during the Rana regime of 104 years (1847–1951). Among other achievements, he is credited with the construction of the Singha Durbar, that stood as the largest palace in South-east Asia until a fire in 1973 destroyed three of its wings. Today, this historic building houses the parliament and other ministries.

Settling into a new home in a foreign country with a different language was rather daunting at first, but her assimilation was eased by the fact that her new Rana family members were passionate connoisseurs of food. Her husband's nanny, Chiniya Champa Didi, initiated her into the marvels of Rana cuisine and taught her everything she knows about Nepali cooking.

As an army wife, she accompanied her husband to foreign countries in the course of his training and to remote villages in Nepal, where he was posted. She had the unique opportunity to learn and absorb the diverse flavours and techniques of local, foreign and fusion cuisine.

Her passion for cooking and collecting recipes culminated in the writing of her first book *The Rana Cookbook: Recipes from the Palaces of Nepal*, published by Penguin Random House India and launched on 16 March 2021. The journey of this book was a true labour of love, since it includes the food eaten by her family on an everyday basis. The 136 recipes in this book include rice and *pulao* preparations, various meat, lentil and vegetable curries cooked in a myriad different ways, rich meat barbecues and light vegetable sautées with an accompaniment of chilli tangy *achars* and condiments. Not to be forgotten is a host of mouth-watering desserts. Her extended family helped complete her Rana culinary repertoire by sharing their precious recipes with her. She managed to document quite a few old recipes which might slowly fade away with the passing of the old *bajais* (Brahmin lady cooks) and involve tedious preparation in today's fast-paced world. Vir Sanghvi, a well-known Indian food curator and critic, praised her work and said: 'This book is to stay for a long time!'

Her *Rana Cookbook* has been nominated for the International Gourmand Award and was featured second in the list of the Ten Best Cookbooks in India by the *Times of India*.

During the pandemic, as her first book lay in a state of incubation for ten months, languishing at the publishers, waiting for the world to get 'normal' again, the idea of a second book to celebrate the vibrant culinary traditions of the diverse Nepalese ethnic communities germinated and gradually flowered. How could she leave the main Nepalese regional communities out of her culinary spectrum?

King Prithvi Narayan Shah laid the foundation for Nepal as we know it today, a remarkable tapestry of multiple communities intermingling with each other. Influenced by China in the north and India in the south, it forms a beautifully synthesized culture assimilating the best elements from both to define a unique identity. The geographic and climatic conditions of these communities are at the root of Nepal's distinct flavours and the vast array of gastronomical delights.

Writing this book has led her into the most interesting alleyways of Nepal's kitchens—from the high mountains, hills and valleys to the Terai jungles—researching, tasting, cooking and finally documenting the recipes that showcase the essence of the cuisine of these communities. In her exploration, she discovered not only culinary delights but also rituals, festivals, fabrics and jewellery that fascinated her. Her humble attempt to present this rich cultural heritage just scratches the surface of the legacy this country upholds. Despite the distinct cultural differences, the various ethnic communities live together in peace and syncretic harmony. We in Nepal pray together, feast together and therefore, stay together!

INTRODUCTION
1

RECIPES 1-8
SHERPA
11

RECIPES 9-19
THAKALI
31

RECIPES 20-40
THAKURI/
BAHUN/
CHETRI/
KHAS
51

RECIPES 41-43
TAMANG
103

RECIPES 44-46
MAGAR
111

RECIPES 47-50
GURUNG
119

RECIPES 51-60
NEWAR
135

RECIPES 61-66
RAI &
LIMBU
165

RECIPES 67-74
THARU
179

RECIPES 75-83

MADESH
195

RECIPES 84-88

MITHILA
217

RECIPES 89-108

MOMOS
233

NEPALI-ENGLISH TERMS
288

LIST OF RECIPES
289

ACKNOWLEDGEMENTS
293

SPECIAL THANKS
294

Contents

Menu Preparation for
King Prithivi Narayan Shah
'Father of the Nation'

नेपालको सिन्की लुटी
मेरगुको घी ले भुटी
पाल्पाको ल्याउ हिड जिरो
रिसिङको ल्याउ पिरो
तनहुको भातसित भीरको दालसित
कन्चर कटौरा भरी
पुरब मोहडा गरी
महाराजको जिउनार बनाउ है

Having taken sinki (fermented radish) from Nepal
Having fried it in butter from Magarant
Bring heeng (asafoetida) from Palpa
Bring the heat of chilli from Jiri
With rice from Tanahu and pulses from Birkot.

In golden bowl and golden platter
Seated on astha dal chowki
(Lotus-shaped stool with eight petals)
With a jug filled with water from the holy Ganges
Face towards the east and prepare His Majesty's food.

Verse written by poet Gyan Dil Das
Translated into English by Poonam R.L. Rana

A Culinary Journey

INTRO

ODUCTION

The bewitchingly beautiful country of Nepal lies nestled between the two populous mammoths, India and China, and has been referred to as the 'Yam between two stones'. Its northern region boasts the spectacular Himalayas, spanning from west

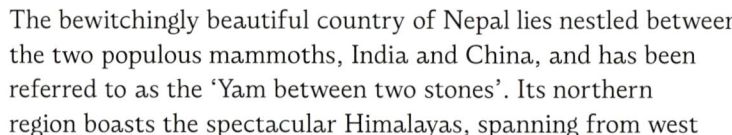

to east, rising to touch the skies, creating a natural crown of white-peaked mountains. Sagarmatha, known in English as Mount Everest, is the highest mountain in the world, shining like the largest diamond in the middle of this beautiful, sparkling tiara. Eight of the highest mountain peaks of the world lie in this heavenly arc. The Himalayan mountain range gives way to the lower-lying hills, interspersed with gentle sloping valleys, criss-crossed with gurgling, gushing rivers and streams. These hills ease into emerald-green slopes and valleys of the mid-Chure range, to finally end in the abundant tropical jungles and fertile plains of the Terai, teeming with diverse flora and fauna.

Nepal is a heterogeneous nation that bears the imprint of its northern and southern neighbours, exquisitely synthesized into a cultural melting pot.

Hinduism, Buddhism, Shaivism and a splatter of other religions, which include Islam, Christianity and Shamanism, coexist peacefully, enriching each other's religious practices and festivals.

The influence of Tibet is evident in the northern region, where Buddhism flourishes, and beautiful monasteries, stupas and *chaityas* (a place of worship), honour the landscape. The air resonates with the chanting of mantras, the flapping of prayer flags and the rhythmic rotation of prayer wheels, echoing the sacred words 'Om Mani Padme Hum', meaning 'praise to the jewel in the lotus'.

In contrast, the western, eastern and southern regions of Nepal share a border with India, and bear the influence of its proximity. The Terai, mainly, has retained much of the southern neighbours' flavour in language, culture and communal customs. The heart of the Nepal Mandala is the Kathmandu Valley, the convergence of north and south, dominated by the rich Newari community, whose roots trace back to the Licchavi era. These Hindu and Buddhist communities are responsible for building temples and monuments of great artistry and expertise, many of which feature in the list of the UNESCO World Heritage Sites.

In eastern Nepal, the Kirati tribes trace their ancestry to Indo-Tibetan influences and have their own unique practices which are distinct from other regions. These contrasting communities live together in harmony, embodying a powerful message of unity in diversity.

Most of the people in Nepal live in extremely drastic and challenging geographical environments. They follow diverse social practices and religions and all these factors influence their food culture and eating habits. This diversity is reflected in the variety of food and beverages prepared in various ways according to their ethnic origin, preparation and shelf life. Means of communication have opened up recently and made life easier, with the accessibility of goods from other regions. But in the old days, these communities survived on the local produce, the grains and vegetables they grew or foraged from the forests, and the animals they hunted or livestock they bred. In the mountainous region, there was no fresh produce for months during the winter season, giving rise to the practices of drying, smoking and fermenting meat and vegetables. There is a wide variety of fermented food that is available and consumed copiously in Nepal. This practice of fermenting is not only resourceful and practical in storing food but is also considered healthy, boosting the immune system and improving digestion.

चार जात
छत्तीस वर्णको
फुलबारी

A garden of four castes and thirty-six ethnic groups

Famous words by
King Prithivi Narayan Shah

3

I have divided Nepal laterally into three regions to assist the reader in understanding the influence of topography on the ethnic communities. The first is the Himalayan mountainous region which stretches from the north-west to north-east Nepal, home to the Sherpas and Thakalis, who trace their ancestry to Mongoloid origins. The second is the lower mountain ranges and hilly areas inhabited by the Thakuri, Khas, Bahun Chetris, Magars, Tamangs, Gurungs, Newars, Rai and Limbu communities, respectively, residing in the region spanning from western Nepal to the mid-section and then towards the east. This segment traces their ancestry to the Aryans mainly, with a sprinkling of Mongoloid and Kirati genes in the east. Finally, the Terai region, which is inhabited by the Tharus in the west, Madeshis in the mid-Terai section, and the Bhojpuris and Mithila Madeshis in the east, who are of Aryan descent. Since the climatic conditions of the communities residing in each lateral area are similar, their food habits are also similar.

Each ethnic community in Nepal brews its own alcohol out of the grain that is grown in that region, be it rice, millet or barley. The dietary habits were mainly influenced by the geographic and climatic conditions of the area in which the community resided. Food consumed every day differed from the special dishes painstakingly prepared for festivals and occasions like births, weddings and mourning. The consumption of alcohol is a very important aspect of everyday life as well as during festivities. Considerable amounts of *rakshi, aila, tongba, jaand, nigaar, kodo, chyang,* etc. are consumed on an everyday basis and during festivals and religious ceremonies. All the special drinks and food are prepared and offered first to the deities amongst much revelry and pageantry, and thereafter consumed copiously, having garnered the blessings of the gods! Women were mainly in the kitchens cooking the food, while the men helped in hunting and preparing the smoked or cooked meat on open fires. Dassain, Lhosar and Maghi, the largest festivals of the Nepalese, are a time for the family to come together to garner the blessings of the elders. Everyone assembles around the hearth in the kitchen to join in the preparation for the festival, food being the most important element of the festivities.

Food, glorious food! I humbly attempted to gather the knowledge of the various recipes prepared and consumed by some of the main ethnic communities of Nepal. It has been a formidable task since the richness of the culture and social practices of the people of Nepal are astoundingly vast and I have barely been able to touch the tip of the iceberg. My journey has taken me through Nepal's kaleidoscope of different ethnic communities, researching and communicating with people proudly interested in conserving their heritage, whether in the form of art and culture or in the very salient form of cuisine. I have tried to assimilate artefacts, utensils and fabric utilized by different ethnic communities as a backdrop for the food imagery. In an attempt to depict the rich cultural heritage, I have also incorporated pieces of indigenous jewellery and costumes worn by the women of the various ethnicities. Similar to my journey in my first book, *The Rana Cookbook: Recipes from the Palaces of Nepal*, I have tried, while walking down the cobbled pathways of this book, to preserve old and forgotten recipes of various ethnic communities. It would be impossible to pen down all the recipes of each community, so with great difficulty, I have chosen the ones that are the most popular and easily replicated. The book strives to depict and throw light on the composite culture and social fabric of various ethnicities through the delectable conduit of food.

108

The number 108 resonates with the mystery spanning across centuries, binding the knowledge of mathematics, science, Vedic cosmology, astrology, numerology, Ayurveda and nearly all the major religions into it. It has been revered as an auspicious number for thousands of years, assimilated in many spiritual traditions and holds special significance in prayer and meditation.

According to Vedic cosmology, the number 108 is the basis of Creation, representing the universe and all of our existence. The great Hindu mantras are chanted 108 times, there are 108 Vedic texts of the Upanishads, 108 beads in our prayer *malas,* the distance between the sun and the moon to the earth is 108 times the diameter of each of these planets.

In Ayurveda, there are 108 *marma* points or vital forces of energy in the body; by performing 108 repetitions of yoga asanas, one activates the 108 *naadi* (pulse) or energy lines, converging at the heart chakra, the main energy centre in our bodies.

The significance and connotations of the number 108 extend far and wide, and fill pages upon pages. However, in this book, its significance lies in its auspicious nature. Given its scientific, spiritual and astrological significance, I hope that with this auspicious number, my book will succeed in offering a higher level of insight into Nepalese cuisine and culture.

Astha Mangal

THE DHARMACHAKRA *(khor-lo/chakra)*

This wheel of life was set in motion by Gautam Buddha's first discourse and signifies the auspiciousness of his teachings and the perpetual turning of the golden wheel of Dharma and life. There is no end or beginning to Dharma and once set in motion, it dissipates ignorance.

THE LOTUS *(padma/padma)*

This beautiful flower depicts a picture of purity and perfect beauty rising above the muddy water of life and strife in which it grows and breeds. Therefore, it achieves a peaceful mental existence, fighting all the desecrations of the physical body.

THE ENDLESS KNOT *(dpal be'u/srivatsa)*

This auspicious endless knot denotes the continuous intermingling of cause and effect, simplicity and harmony in life. It is a symbol of unity in all things material and spiritual, and the interdependence of methodology and wisdom.

THE PARASOL *(gdugs/chattra)*

The parasol denotes protection, physically, from heat and rain. Spiritually, it signifies shade from the inclemency of life like disease and vicissitudes of fortune. The parasol in the old times was a symbol of power, figuratively seeking protection under the shade of auspiciousness and spirituality.

The word *Asthamangala* signifies the eight auspicious symbols common to three religions, Hinduism, Buddhism and Jainism. They are the symbolic attributes or energy points that teach us the path to enlightenment. They are the symbols of good fortune and adorn gateways to temples, places and homes. In this book the placement of *asthamangala* signs are in no way associated with any ethnic community; they are just beautiful lucky charms to enable this book's smooth journey through the ages.

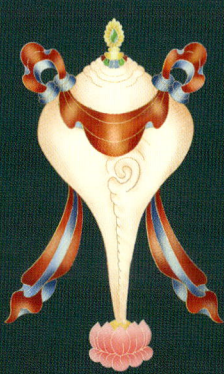

THE CONCH *(dung g.yas-'khil/daksinavartasankha)*

The right-facing conch shell is an instrument whose sound resonates to announce important meetings or rituals, trumpet a call to war or herald victory in battle. At a deeper spiritual level, the sound of the conch shell reverberates to signify the victory of good over evil as well as awakening of the inner self to spiritualism and the right path.

PAIR OF GOLDEN FISH *(gser-nya/suvarnamstya)*

The pair of golden fish symbolize complete happiness and freedom of movement, fertility and fearlessness. They denote the courage in humans as they swim freely through the sea of life overcoming all the challenges and finding happiness and abundance.

THE VICTORY BANNER *(rgyalan/dhwaja)*

This victory sign flies high over temples and homes, denoting the victory of life over fear of death, knowledge over ignorance and the ultimate attainment of peace. It symbolizes the victory over negativity and challenges in life.

THE TREASURE VASE *(gter-chen-po'i bum-pa/kalasha)*

This treasure vase depicts abundance in material as well as spiritual attributes. It is symbolic of longevity and wisdom. It basically signifies a fulfillment of material and spiritual desires.

SHERPA

The famous Sherpa community hails from the mountainous region in Tibet and even further, in Mongolia, migrating to settle in the Sagarmatha (Everest) area of the Solukhumbu valley. *Sherpa* means, people from the east. From their traditional home, they spread out over the eastern hill districts and have earned a glorious name in the history of global mountaineering as the most hardy and resilient people. After the epic scaling of Mt Everest by Tenzing Norgay and Edmund Hillary in 1953, the Sherpa community has catapulted into prominence as mountaineers and guides and their economy has been vastly uplifted thanks to their skills. Having lived in this mountainous region for years, they are naturally acclimatized to great physical feats at high altitudes, carrying heavy loads and scaling high mountains without the use of oxygen. Pasang Lhamu Sherpa became the first Nepali woman to scale Mt Everest in 1993; she unfortunately died on the slopes during her descent.

The Sherpas retain much from their Tibetan heritage but have integrated well into the Nepali mainstream. They are devout Buddhists and have built beautiful monasteries all over the Khumbu region. The most famous being Tengboche, nestling in the oldest Sherpa village in Nepal, one of the highest monasteries in the world, resplendent with beautiful paintings and *thangkas*. *Lhosar,* Tibetan New Year, is celebrated with singing, dancing and copious amounts of feasting.

One of the Sherpas' main occupations is animal husbandry of yak, mountain sheep and cattle, grazing them on the alpine grassland slopes. They engage in sporadic farming, growing cereals like maize, barley and wheat, vegetables like potato, radish and beans—these are the staple foods of the Sherpas. Their food culture is similar to Tibet's, but they have assimilated their own traditional dishes such as fresh and dried yak meat, hand-pulled noodles, potato preparations, steaming radish and bean stews, which are delicious and keep them snug and warm during the cold climate of their region.

Rilduk

Kur

Aaloo Phing

Shyakpa

Kur

Sherpa Flat Bread

Preparation time: 30 minutes
Serves: 8

INGREDIENTS

2 cups plain flour
1 tbsp. baking powder
½ tbsp. salt
water

PREPARATION

Mix all the ingredients and knead into a smooth dough, cover and let it rest for ½ hour. Divide into equal-sized balls and roll out into ¼-inch thick discs. Cook in a warm pan on both sides until they turn golden brown. Serve topped with yak butter.

Rilduk

Sherpa Potato Soup

Preparation time: 30 minutes
Serves: 8

INGREDIENTS

2 tbsp. ghee
6 boiled potatoes
1 sliced onion
2-3 chopped tomatoes
5 cloves garlic
3-4 red chillies
1 cup grated cheese
20 timur seeds
½ cup chopped green onions
Salt to taste

PREPARATION

Boil and grate the potatoes, place in a large wooden mortar, keep pounding till their elasticity is seen, keep aside. Heat oil and sauté the onions till a light golden brown. Crush the *timur* seeds, garlic and red chillies in a mortar and pestle to a coarse consistency. Add this ground mixture to the oil and cook for 2-3 minutes. Add the chopped tomatoes to the pan and stir for 2 minutes. Add salt, water and chopped green onions to the soup and cook till it boils. Make small balls of the potato mixture and add to the boiling soup. Cook till the balls float on top of the liquid. Add the grated cheese, let it melt, serve hot!

Aaloo Phing

Potato Curry with Glass Noodles

This recipe was originally prepared with yak meat, now buff is more commonly used.

Preparation time: 45 minutes
Serves: 6

INGREDIENTS

1 cup meat cubes with bones (optional)
2 cups potatoes cut into cubes
1 cup carrots cut into cubes
1 tsp. garlic paste
1 tsp. ginger paste
2 tbsp. chopped onions
25 g phing noodles
1 tsp. coriander powder
1 tsp. cumin powder
½ tsp. chilli flakes
½ tsp. turmeric powder
2 tbsp. oil
Salt to taste

PREPARATION

Soak the noodles in hot water for 15 minutes. Heat the oil in a pan and add chopped onions, garlic and ginger paste, sauté for 2 minutes. Add the meat, chopped potatoes and carrots and dry spices, stir for 2 minutes till the vegetables are well coated with the oil and spices. Add 2 cups of water and cover and cook on medium heat till the meat and potatoes are cooked. Add the noodles, cook for a further 5 minutes, serve hot, garnished with chopped green onions. Any meat of your choice like yak, beef, chicken or mutton can be used.

4

Shyakpa/Thukpa

Sherpa Soup

Shyakpa and thukpa are Sherpa soups, very similar in taste and ingredients. The main difference between them being that shyakpa is made out of thick hand-pulled noodles of different shapes, while thukpa is spicier and made out of long and thin spaghetti-like noodles. This hot, wholesome soup is perfect on a cold, wintry evening.

Preparation time: 45 minutes
Serves: 6-8

INGREDIENTS

HANDMADE NOODLES
2 cups refined flour
1 tbsp. oil
Water

SOUP
2 cups yak sukuti or fresh yak/mutton meat
1 cup potatoes
½ cup carrots
½ cup radish
1 bunch bak choy
½ cup sliced onions
2 tbsp. coarsely ground ginger
4 tbsp. coarsely ground garlic
1 tbsp. coarsely ground red chillies
½ tsp. turmeric powder
3 tbsp. oil
Salt to taste

GARNISH
Green onions
Chilli oil
Timur chope

PREPARATION

Make smooth dough out of the flour, water and oil, like one would for *momos;* keep aside. Chop the meat and vegetables into 1 inch cubes. Heat oil and sauté the roughly crushed garlic and ginger, add the sliced onions with a pinch of turmeric powder. Once the onions are translucent, add the *sukuti* or meat and cook till it is brown. Add all the vegetables, except the *bak choy* and cook for a few minutes. Add water or stock and cook till meat and vegetables are half-cooked, add the handmade noodles, breaking off pieces of the rolled out dough to your preferred size. Just before serving, add the *bak choy* and cook for 2 minutes. Garnish with chilli oil and green onions.

THUKPA

Use thin noodles and chop the vegetables small, use minced meat instead of meat cubes or *sukuti.* This soup is spicier than *Shyakpa* so add chillies and *timur chope* (sichuan pepper powder) according to your taste.

Rikikur

Potato Pancake

In the Sherpa language, 'riki' means potatoes and 'kur' means bread.

Preparation time: 30 minutes
Serves: 8

INGREDIENTS

10 finely grated potatoes
4 tbsp. buckwheat/refined flour
2 eggs
Salt to taste
Oil for frying

INGREDIENTS FOR ACHAR

½ cup red chillies
1 cup garlic cloves
Salt to taste

PREPARATION

Finely grate the potatoes in a circular motion. Mix the flour, salt and eggs and whisk together until well integrated and smooth, add water to make a smooth consistency. Heat a nonstick pan and brush with oil, pour enough batter into the pan to make a medium-thick pancake. Cook till golden brown and flip and cook the other side as well. Serve hot with yak butter, red chilli *achar* and fresh green onion chutney.

ACCOMPANIED BY

Red Chilli Achar
(Red Chilli Pickle)

Mix together and grind to a fine paste. This pickle is hot!

Shyaphale

Deep-Fried Minced Meat Patties

Preparation time: 30 minutes
Serves: 4-6

INGREDIENTS

2 cups refined flour (maida)
½ cup water
Chicken, pork or beef filling
Oil for frying

FILLING

½ kg minced chicken/pork/buff
2 tbsp. finely chopped onions
2 tbsp. chopped green onions
1 tbsp. chopped garlic
1 tsp. red chilli powder/flakes
Salt to taste

INGREDIENTS FOR ACHAR

2 large stalks scallions (green onions)
4 cloves garlic
2 green chillies
½ cup thick sour cream or yogurt
Salt to taste

PREPARATION

Mix all the ingredients for the filling and marinate for half an hour. Knead the flour and water into a firm dough, keep aside for half an hour. Roll into large discs, place 2 tbsp. of the filling mixture of your choice in half of the disc, roll one side over and cover the filling into a half moon shape, crimp the edges and make into a crescent shape. Deep-fry on slow heat and serve hot.

ACCOMPANIED BY

Green Onion Achar

(Scallion/Green Onion Pickle)

Chop and add the green onions, garlic, chillies and salt to a blender and make a smooth paste, add to the sour cream or yogurt and mix well. You can use mayonnaise if sour cream and yogurt are unavailable.

Preparation time: 15 minutes
Serves 6

7

Khapse

Traditional Sherpa Biscuits

Preparation time: 30 minutes
Serves: 10

INGREDIENTS

2 cups refined flour
50 grams butter
3 tsp. sugar
1 tsp. salt
1 ½ cups water

PREPARATION

Mix the sugar in water till it dissolves; mix all the ingredients in a bowl and knead together to make a soft dough. Keep aside to rest for half an hour. Roll out a disc of ¼ inch thickness and cut out the edges and make a square shape.

DIFFERENT SHAPES

1. Leave the edges and cut ½ inch thin strips diagonally, cut ½ inch slit in the middle and gently pull one edge through the opening.
2. Cut the square in half and make a cylindrical shape and press the edges. Flatten a little and make 2 inch cuts on one side, open and separate cuts, pinch the top and criss-cross each segment. Make big or small cylinders according to preference.
3. Cut the same way as described in *2* and put one strip into the other and overlap.

When all the patterns are made, heat oil and fry to a deep golden colour. You can store the *khapse* in an airtight container for up to a month and serve with butter tea.

Phapchung

Butter Tea

Preparation time: 20 minutes
Serves: 4

INGREDIENTS

200 grams Chinese tea
2 ½ cups milk
2 cups water
250 grams butter
1 tsp. salt

PREPARATION

Boil tea in water for 10-15 minutes, strain and add milk, butter and salt. Place in a blender or *dhongmu* (wooden vessel to make tea), blend and serve hot.

THAKALI

The Thakali community originated from Thak Khola, a high valley of the Kali Gandaki river stretching across the Annapurna and Dhaulagiri mountains. It's in this region that one finds the transition from the mid-hilly region of Hindu Nepal to the Buddhist high mountains, bordering the northern borders of the country. They have spread from Jomsom in the north, Pokhara in the mid region to as far as Bhairawa in the south. The Thakali town of Tukuche, a Tibetan term meaning 'the salt-trading grounds' became famous as the nexus for trading. The community developed their trading skills, migrating to other regions of the country to further their business prowess. The Thakalis follow a blend of Buddhism, Bon-Po, Jhankrism and Hinduism, which formerly originated from Jhankrism, a Shamanistic cult, which was their original religion.

The Tangbetani Gurung community lives in just two villages in the Jomsom area. Their cuisine is influenced mainly by the indigenous Thakali community but has retained the original Gurung flavour and has created a blended form of cuisine. This community is a typical example of assimilation of different ethnic cultures. Barley, wheat, buckwheat, maize, radish and potatoes are their main produce.

The *Thakali thaali* has made its mark in the arena of Nepali cuisine and has gained great popularity in the last few years. The sizzling sound and smell of hot *ghee* being poured over rice or buckwheat *dhindo* (porridge), *kanchemba* (crispy buckwheat fries), famous Mustang *daal* (lentils), *sukuti* (dried yak meat), Mustang potatoes served with a heavy dash of *timur chope* (sichuan pepper powder). An accompaniment of healthy mustard greens served with spicy radish pickle makes the palate tingle and transports one straight to the beautiful mountains and valleys of Thak Khola.

Kanchemba

Buckwheat Fries

Traditionally, the Thakalis used ghee to fry these buckwheat fingers.

Preparation time: 45 minutes
Serves: 6

INGREDIENTS

1 ½ cups buckwheat flour
2 cups water
1 tbsp. ghee
1 cup oil/ghee for frying
Salt to taste

PREPARATION

Bring 2 cups of water to a boil in a pot, add salt to it, add the flour gradually, stirring constantly with a wooden spatula or spoon. Turn the heat down and add the *ghee*. Keep stirring till it forms into a smooth *dhindo* (sticky dough). Cool the *dhindo* till it is warm to the touch. Grease your palms and place a small ball between your palms, roll it to form a small finger with tapering ends. Heat the oil/ *ghee* and deep-fry the buckwheat fingers till crisp. Serve with *timur chope* or tomato pickle.

10

Phapar Ko Dhindo

Buckwheat Porridge

Preparation time: 20 minutes
Serves: 4

INGREDIENTS

1 cup buckwheat flour
4 cups water
1 tbsp. ghee
1 tsp. timur chope
Method 2, pg 45

PREPARATION

Heat the water in a thick deep pot or originally *kasaundi*; when boiling, add the buckwheat flour and stir vigorously with a wooden ladle till there are no lumps (originally a wooden stick was used to stir the porridge). Keep stirring till all the water is absorbed and it looks like a thick porridge, then add ½ cup of water and stir to mix well. Serve piping hot in the middle of the platter and make an indentation with the back of a spoon; pour the hot *ghee* in the centre and sprinkle with the *timur chope*.

Dodo

Wheat Flour Balls with Spices

Preparation time: 30 minutes
Serves: 6

INGREDIENTS

½ kg wheat flour
½ cup mustard oil
1 onion
3-4 crushed garlic cloves
½ tsp. turmeric powder
½ tsp. chilli powder
Salt to taste

PREPARATION

Make a dough out of the water and flour, keep aside for 10 minutes. Heat the water and break small round lumps of dough into the water, cook till they float on top, drain and keep in a plate. Heat oil in a wok and add the crushed garlic and chopped onions, sauté for 2 minutes, add the dodo pieces and spices and sauté for five minutes. Serve hot.

Mula Theeche Ko Achar

Pla

Ngyoshol

Bhatta

Ghinti

Phapar Ko Dhindo

Dodo

12

Bhatta

Dried Colocasia and Black Soya Bean Soup

Preparation time: 30 minutes
Serves: 4

INGREDIENTS

½ cup black soya beans
¼ cup dried colocasia leaves/
chopped fresh leaves (optional)
2 tbsp. ghee
4 coarsely crushed garlic cloves
1 tbsp. barley flour
½ tsp. red chilli powder
½ tsp. turmeric powder
Salt to taste

PREPARATION

Heat *ghee* in a deep pot or pressure cooker and roast the black soya beans in it for 2 minutes, add the dried colocasia leaf powder and crushed garlic and stir for 2 minutes. Add the rest of the spices, salt and barley flour to it and stir for 3 minutes, then add 3 cups of water. Cover the lid and cook for 15 minutes. The soup should be of a thin, liquid consistency. Serve hot.

Ghinti

Dried Blood Sausage

Preparation time: 30 minutes
Serves: 10

INGREDIENTS

4 cups ragati (fresh blood)
1 whole garlic bulb
3 tsp. jimbu (mountain allium)
½ cup yak minced meat with fat
½ cup minced offals
Salt to taste

PREPARATION

Coarsely grind the garlic and mix all the ingredients and stuff into clean, well-washed sheep/goat intestines. Cook in water for 10 minutes. Hang the sausages to dry and store in a dark, dry place. When ready to eat, heat oil and sauté in the pan, add salt and turmeric powder. Grill on all sides, cut into 2 inch pieces and serve. You can add the sausages to *Mustang kaalo daal*.

Pla

Potato, Bean and Sukuti/Dried Meat Curry

Preparation time: 45 minutes
Serves: 6

INGREDIENTS

4 potatoes
1 cup sukuti (dried yak/mutton meat)
250 grams beans
½ cup mustard oil
½ cup sliced onions
1 tsp. jimbu (mountain allium)
½ tsp. turmeric powder
1 tsp. red chilli powder
Salt to taste

PREPARATION

Heat oil in a clay pot (if available) and add *jimbu* and chopped onions; sauté for 2 minutes. Add the beans, potatoes and *sukuti* and cook for 5 minutes. Add the spices and stir till the beans are well-coated, add 2-3 cups water and cover for 20 minutes. In the old days, they would slow cook the curry using a flat stone as a lid so the ingredients would cook well. If cooking in a pressure cooker, cook for 2 whistles and leave covered for 10 minutes.

Ngyoshol

Wild Goosefoot Spinach and Yogurt

Bethu spinach goes by many names such as bethu, wild goosefoot, lamb's quarters, melde and fat-hen. If not available, you could use young amaranth leaves.

Preparation time: 20 minutes
Serves: 4

INGREDIENTS

1 bunch Bethu saag (wild goosefoot/wild spinach)
2 cups yogurt
1 cup chopped cilantro
2 green chillies
2 cloves garlic
1 tsp. red chillies
Salt to taste

PREPARATION

Grind together all ingredients except *saag* and yogurt to a fine paste. Chop and cook the *Bethu saag* in a little water until wilted, squeeze out the water and keep aside. Whisk the yogurt till smooth and mix all the ingredients together. Serve cold.

16

Mula Theeche Ko Achar

Crushed Radish Fresh Pickle

Preparation time: 15 minutes
Serves: 6

INGREDIENTS

1 large radish
2 tbsp. coriander leaves
3 garlic cloves
1 tsp. red chilli powder
1 tsp. jadi buti/paan septi (looks like fennel seeds)
1 tsp. heated oil
Salt to taste

PREPARATION

Cut the radish in big pieces and crush coarsely with a pestle and mortar, add all the other ingredients and mix well. Serve with a dash of lemon accompanying a Thakali meal. This fresh pickle is the best accompaniment to a Thakali meal.

Timur Chope

Sichuan Pickle

Preparation time: 20 minutes
Makes: 1 bottle

INGREDIENTS 1

3 tbsp. timur (sichuan pepper)
1 cup red chillies
1 tbsp. jwano (oregano)
Salt/rock salt to taste

INGREDIENTS 2

2 tbsp. timur
4 tbsp. red chillies/dried akhabari khursani
(red cherry pepper chilli)
1 cup coarsely ground garlic
3 tbsp. sesame seeds
2 tbsp. chuk amilo (concentrate of lemon)
½ cup mustard oil
Salt to taste

PREPARATION

METHOD 1
Dry roast all ingredients in a pan together, except the salt. Cool completely and grind in a mortar and pestle or grinder to a coarse powder, add salt to taste.

METHOD 2
Dry roast the chillies, *timur* and sesame seeds separately and grind coarsely, (break the chillies in half when cool and shake out the seeds if wanting a milder *chope*). Coarsely grind the garlic, heat the mustard oil till it smokes and fry the garlic a light golden brown. Remove from heat and mix all the ingredients, consume immediately or cool and store in a bottle; keep refrigerated for further use.

Timur

Timur Chope

Jimbu

Sukuti Hale Ko Kaalo Bodi Daal

Mustang Aaloo

18

Mustang Aaloo

Mustang Potatoes

Preparation time: 45 minutes
Serves: 6

INGREDIENTS

1 kg Mustang potatoes/red potatoes
½ cup ghee
1 tsp. fenugreek seeds
½ tsp. turmeric powder
1 tsp. timur seeds
4 red chillies/1 tsp. chilli flakes
Salt to taste

PREPARATION

Parboil and peel the potatoes; the skin can be retained if preferred, for a healthier option. Chop the potatoes in thick cubes. Coarsely grind the *timur* and red chillies and keep aside. Heat the *ghee* and temper with the fenugreek seeds, and fry till they turn dark, add the *timur* and red chilli and turmeric powder to the hot *ghee* and fry for 1 minute, add the potatoes and salt and stir on medium heat till the potatoes are coated with the spicy *ghee* and cooked through. Serve piping hot.

Sukuti Hale' Ko Kaalo Bodi Daal

Mustang Lentils with Dried Yak Meat

The daal was slow-cooked in an iron pot originally and turned black in colour.

Preparation time: 30 minutes
Serves: 6

INGREDIENTS

2 cups Mustang daal/simi
1 cup dried yak meat (optional)
4 cups water
½ tsp. turmeric powder
½ tsp. ginger paste
½ tsp. garlic paste
2 tsp. ghee
2 ½ tbsp. jimbu

PREPARATION

Wash the *daal* well and place all the ingredients except the *ghee* and *jimbu* in a pressure cooker and cook for 4 whistles. Pour the contents into an iron pot and cook further till the colour turns black. Heat the *ghee* and temper with the *jimbu,* pour over the *daal* and serve hot.

VEGETARIAN OPTION
Omit the dried meat and cook in the same way.

THAKURI/ BAHUN/ CHETRI/ KHAS

The Bahuns (Brahmans) and Chetris (Kshatriyas) are two different castes that originated from the Khas ethnic group of Nepal, with their origins tracing back to the Indo-Aryan tribes of South Asia. They migrated to the western hills of Nepal mainly after the foreign invasions in the Indian subcontinent, slowly spreading through the length and breadth of the country. Together, they constitute the largest ethnic group and can be found spread over fifteen districts of Nepal. The Thakuris are the aristocracy among this community and enjoy the highest social and political status. The Shah Kings, the former kings of Nepal originating from Gorkha, belong to this clan. The descendants of the Khasa Malla Kings ruled the Baise and Chaubise principalities of western Nepal. They occupy high social status, their main occupation being either agriculture or government service. The ruling elite of the country has originated from this community and was directly responsible for the unification of Nepal; they continue to hold dominance in the handling of government affairs. The scions of the different castes include Brahmans, Thakuris, Ranas, Thapas, Pandes, Basnyats, Bohra, Mahat, Dhami, Rawal and a few others. The Bahun Chetris are Hindus and their important festivals are Dassain (Dusshera or Durga Puja) and Tihar (Diwali), which they follow with rituals and festivities, indulging in days of praying, feasting and merriment.

The main cuisine of this ethnic community is what is synonymous with Nepali food, mainly *daal, bhaat, tarkari, masu, achar* (lentils, rice, vegetables, meat and pickles). A staggering amount of preparations are made out of these ingredients. Many of the popular dishes of this community have already been included in my first book and are thus missing from this one. There is a great variety of lentils, different types of rice, wheat, millet, barley and buckwheat, seasonal vegetables, meat, fresh and fermented pickles. No Nepali sleeps well without a meal of their favourite *daal bhaat* nestling snugly in their stomachs.

Dupka

Tarkari
Hale Ko
Kadi/Palyo

54

Chaulani

Gatani Daal Ko Dupka/Palyo

20

Dupka

Lentil Ball Soup

This tasty lentil soup is famous in the hilly area of western Nepal. In the old days, a coin would be hidden inside some of the dupka balls and the person whose platter it was discovered in, would be considered bhagyamani (lucky). This preparation was usually cooked during shraadh (day of homage to one's ancestors).

Preparation time: 45 minutes
Serves: 8

INGREDIENTS

1 cup gahat daal (horse gram lentils)
1 cup maas daal (black gram beans)
1 tbsp. wheat flour
1 ½ tsp. coriander powder
1 ½ tsp. cumin powder
1 ½ tsp. red chilli powder
¼ tsp. timur powder
2 tsp. chuk amilo (concentrate of lemon juice)
or lemon juice
Salt to taste

TEMPERING

2 tbsp. ghee
2 tsp. jimbu (mountain allium)
1 tbsp. roughly ground ginger
1 tbsp. roughly ground garlic
1 ½ tsp. coriander powder
1 ½ tsp. cumin powder
1 ½ tsp. red chilli powder
¼ tsp. turmeric powder
Salt to taste

PREPARATION

Soak the *maas daal* overnight, wash and grind to a thick paste. Dry roast the *gahat daal* in a heavy-bottomed pan for 2-3 minutes then add ½ cup hot water and cook. Separate half of the *maas daal* paste in a bowl, add 1 tbsp. of wheat flour and 3 cups of water and make into a thin gruel. Add to the pot of cooking *daal*. Stir continuously making sure there are no lumps. When the gruel thickens add all the spices, salt and *chuk amilo*. Add 2 cups of water and simmer again for 10 minutes until the *daal* is cooked, add more water and make the *daal* into a thin consistency. Now take the thick batter of *maas daal,* add salt and mix well and drop small *dupka* balls gently into the *daal* soup. Cook without stirring for 5 minutes until the *dupka* balls float to the surface, boil for a further 5 minutes and make sure the *daal* soup is a thin consistency. Heat *ghee* in another tempering pan, add all the tempering ingredients and cook till a nice golden brown, pour over the *daal* and serve piping hot. Garnish with chopped coriander.

Gatani Daal Ko Dupka/Palyo

Horse Gram Lentils Cooked in Buttermilk

Preparation time: 45 minutes
Serves: 8

INGREDIENTS

2 cups gahat daal (horse gram lentils)
4 ½ cups yogurt
2 tbsp. ghee
2 tbsp. rice flour
1 tsp. cumin seeds
1 cup sliced onions
1 tsp. garlic paste
1 tsp. ginger paste
1 tsp. turmeric powder
1 tsp. cumin powder
1 tsp. coriander powder
1 ½ tsp. red chilli powder
Salt to taste
Oil for deep-frying

PREPARATION

Soak the *gahat daal* overnight. Rinse with water and grind coarsely, mix salt and whisk to make a thick batter. Wet the palm of your hand with water, take 1 tbsp. of batter in your hand, make a ball, flatten it and slip into hot oil and deep-fry till golden brown on both sides. Keep aside. In a bowl, place the yogurt, add the rice flour and salt and whisk till smooth. In a pan heat the *ghee* and add the cumin seeds, let them splutter then add the sliced onions and cook till translucent, add the garlic-ginger paste stir till the raw smell dissipates. Add the dry spices: cumin, coriander, turmeric powder and red chillies and cook again adding ½ cup warm water, stir till the *ghee* separates. Turn the heat down then add the yogurt soup gently and mix well. Cook on low heat for 15 minutes and keep stirring so it does not stick to the base of the pan. Add water to fix the consistency. Add the fried dumplings to the hot yogurt soup 10 minutes before serving. Garnish with chopped coriander. Serve hot.

VEGETABLE OPTION
TARKARI HALE KO KADI/PALYO
(Vegetables Cooked in a Yogurt Soup)
Vegetables of your choice like brinjal, radish, spinach or cucumber can be used in the yogurt soup. Make the soup like in the above recipe and add the chopped vegetable of your choice. Simmer until the vegetables are cooked and serve hot.

Chaulani

Tempered Lentil Balls in Rice Starch Water

Preparation time: 30 minutes
Serves: 6

INGREDIENTS

1 cup rice
3 cups chaulani water
2 tbsp. bhaang achar
Juice of 2 lemons
½ tsp. cumin seeds
½ tsp. fenugreek seeds
1 tbsp. mustard oil
Salt to taste

BARA

2 cups maas daal (black-eyed beans)
½ tsp. asafoetida
1 tsp. turmeric powder
Salt to taste

PREPARATION

This dish is usually made while cooking rice. Wash the rice two times and throw the water, the third time you wash the rice, strain and retain the water. This water is called *chaulani*. Take 2 tbsp. of *bhaang achar* (Recipe No. 36) and add the *chaulani* water to it, leave for 10 minutes to let the *bhaang* flavour seep into the water, mix well and strain the water into a bowl. Throw the dregs of the *bhaang* and add the lemon juice to the *chaulani*. While the water is resting with *bhaang* in it grind the *maas daal* coarsely, add the turmeric powder, asafoetida and salt, and whisk well to mix the batter. Oil your hands and keep a spoonful of batter in your hands, make a flat round shape and slip into the hot oil and deep-fry the *baras* to a golden brown. Once they are all fried add to the water. Heat the mustard oil and temper the cumin and fenugreek seeds, add to the *baras* in the *chaulani* and serve.

Khasi Pakuwa

Dahi Hale Ko Macha

22

Bhaddu Ma Pakai Ko Khasi Pakuwa

Mutton Cooked in a Brass Vessel

This dish tastes best cooked in this original style. It is cooked in a brass container called bhaddu, because of the shape of the vessel, it contains the heat within it and facilitates cooking. The mutton meat was cooked with skin and fat originally, but this can be omitted according to personal taste or for a healthier option. Since no water is used in its preparation, it lasts for days without refrigeration.

Preparation time: 2 hours
Serves: 10

INGREDIENTS

2 kg mutton with skin, fat and bones
1 cup mustard oil
1 ½ cup ghee
4 bay leaves
6 big cardamoms
25 small cardamoms
1 tsp. cloves
4 small sticks cinnamon
5 medium-sized onions cut in quarters
⅔ cup whole peeled garlic cloves
⅔ cup ginger cut in round slices
2 tbsp. coriander powder
½ tbsp. cumin powder
1 tbsp. turmeric powder
1 tbsp. red chilli powder
Salt to taste

PREPARATION

Mix all the ingredients, except the whole spices, bay leaves, small and big cardamoms, cloves and cinnamon sticks, with the mutton and add 2 tbsp. oil. Marinate this mutton for 30 min. Heat the mustard oil in a heavy-bottomed pan and fry the whole spices for 2 minutes. Add the marinated mutton and cook covered on low heat for 2 hours, stirring from time to time. The skin of the mutton should also be cooked and soft by the time the mutton is cooked and the oil floats on top. This dish is served either hot or cold and called *jamai ko masu* if served cold because the *ghee* congeals with the meat. During the Dassain festival, this dish is best eaten with *cheura* (beaten rice).

Dahi Hale Ko Macha

Fish Cooked in Yogurt Sauce

Preparation time: 30 minutes
Serves: 6

INGREDIENTS

1 kg Rohu fish
2 cups yogurt
1 cup mustard oil
3 bay leaves
1 cup sliced onions
1 ½ tsp. garlic paste
1 ½ tsp. ginger paste
1 tsp. mustard seeds
1 tsp. coriander powder
1 tsp. cumin powder
3 tsp. red chilli powder
2 tsp. turmeric powder
Salt to taste

PREPARATION

Slice the fish in 1 inch round pieces, mix the fish slices with all the ingredients except oil, bay leaves and mustard seeds. Heat the oil and add the mustard seeds and bay leaves and temper for 1 minute, gently add the fish yogurt mixture to the hot oil, stir and cook on medium heat till the water evaporates, fish is cooked and the oil floats on top.

Mada

Maas Daal Roth

Koiralo Ko Achar

Maas Daal Roth

Bread Stuffed with Black Gram

The original style of cooking the roth would be over a coal fire and serving it with home-made cow/buffalo ghee.

Preparation time: 30 minutes
Serves: 6

INGREDIENTS

1 ½ cups maas daal (black gram lentils)
½ tsp. ginger paste
½ tsp. garlic paste
1 tsp. cumin powder
1 tsp. coriander powder
1 tsp. red chilli powder
1 tbsp. chopped coriander leaves
Oil for deep-frying
Salt to taste

DOUGH

2 cups whole wheat flour
1 cup water
½ tsp. salt

PREPARATION

Soak the lentils overnight in water, drain well and grind coarsely, mix all the ingredients for the filling except oil, and keep aside. Knead the flour with water to a pliable consistency, cover and keep aside for 30 minutes. Make same-sized dough balls, place one on the rolling board and roll to 3 inches width, place in your left palm and place 1 tbsp. of lentil dough in the middle, put the edges together gently, and pinch the ends close so the patty is stuffed with the filling. Sprinkle a little flour on the board and roll gently taking care not to split it. Place aside in a tray, make the other dough balls likewise. Heat a griddle and cook the *roth* on both sides, flip to the first side again and press on it with a folded cloth napkin so it fluffs up and cooks well. A generous helping of *ghee* spread on it makes this bread delicious.

PURI OPTION

Heat oil in a wok and gently slip in each disc and deep-fry to a nice golden brown on both sides.

Mada

Rice Flour Crêpes

Ghee was used in the old days to make this recipe, but oil can be used if preferred.

Preparation time: 30 minutes
Serves: 4

INGREDIENTS

3 cups fine rice flour
½ cup ghee/oil
Sugar (optional)

PREPARATION

Mix the rice flour with water and make a thin fluid consistency. Keep aside for an hour. Heat a *tawa* (griddle) and apply a little *ghee* on the surface, pour one ladle of the batter and spread to as thin a crêpe as you can manage. Heat one side and flip over, apply *ghee* again on entire surface and when cooked, flip over again. Pour another ladle of batter over the first crêpe and cook in the same way as the first. Keep applying *ghee* and layering the crêpe—five layers used to be the norm in the old days but you can make as many as you want. The layers of crêpes can be seen when they are cut in half.

OPTION

Sugar can be sprinkled in between layers if you prefer to have the *mada* as a dessert.

26

Koiralo Ko Achar

Ebony Buds Fresh Pickle

Preparation time: 30 minutes
Serves: 6

INGREDIENTS

½ kg ebony buds
8 green chillies
1 tsp. red chilli powder
½ tsp. timur
Juice of 2 lemons
5 tbsp. bhaang ko achar (Recipe No. 36)
Salt to taste
½ tsp. fenugreek/panch phoran seeds
2 tbsp. mustard oil
1 cup water

PREPARATION

Boil the buds with 5 green chillies till cooked, drain the hot water and put in cold water to retain the colour. Add the chillies, *timur* powder, lemon juice, *bhaang achar* and salt with 1 cup water and mix. Pour over the ebony buds and mix gently. Heat the mustard oil till it smokes and add the *panch phoran*/fenugreek seeds and 5 green chillies slit in half. Take the pan off the fire, add the turmeric powder to the hot oil, swirl and add to the *achar,* mix and serve.

Nesuse

Rice Flour Cake

In the old days, this dish was cooked on a coal fire with coals on the lid to resemble an oven.

Preparation time: 45 minutes
Serves: 8

INGREDIENTS

3 cups coarse rice flour
1 ½ cups sugar
1 cup ghee/butter
3 cups yogurt

PREPARATION

Mix the flour, sugar and butter with your fingertips till the mixture resembles coarse breadcrumbs; slowly add the yogurt and mix again till well integrated. Pour the batter into an oiled cake tin. Place in a heated oven, reduce the heat to medium and cook for 30 minutes.

28

Khasi Masu Gaente Mula Ko Ledo

Radish and Mutton Curry

The original mutton dishes were all cooked with bones, fat and skin.
For healthier options, omit the fat and skin.

Preparation time: 45 minutes
Serves: 6

INGREDIENTS

½ kg mutton with bones
3 cups turnips
1 tbsp. ghee
½ cup mustard oil
½ tsp. fenugreek seeds
½ tsp. carom seeds
½ tsp. cumin seeds
2 red chillies
1 pinch asafoetida
1 tsp. turmeric powder
2 tbsp. chopped garlic
½ cup chopped onions
2 tsp. garlic paste
1 ½ tsp. ginger paste
2 tbsp. onion paste
4 medium chopped tomatoes
1 ½ tbsp. coriander powder
2 tbsp. cumin powder
1 tbsp. red chilli powder
½ tsp. garam masala
½ tsp. ground jaipatri (nutmeg)
Salt to taste
Coriander leaves for garnishing

PREPARATION

Cut mutton and turnip into 1 inch pieces and keep aside. Heat mustard oil till it smokes, add fenugreek, cumin, carom seeds and asafoetida till they change colour, add chopped onions and fry till they change golden. Add the meat, turmeric powder and salt and stir fry till the meat changes colour to a dark brown. Add the turnips and stir fry for 3 minutes on medium heat till tender. Pour in the ground onions, ginger and garlic pastes, mix well, add the dry spices and chopped tomatoes, keep stirring till the oil separates. Add 2 cups water and pressure cook for three whistles. Take the pot off the fire and check when cool that the mutton and radish are tender but retain their shape. Serve hot, garnished with chopped green coriander.

72

Khasi Masu Kauli Kerau

Mutton Cooked with Cauliflower and Peas

Cauliflower has an interesting story of its journey from UK to Nepal. During his visit to London, Prime Minister Jung Bahadur tasted the vegetable and his preference for it was noticed by members of his retinue. As a result, cauliflower seeds accompanied the package of ideas from the UK to modernize Nepal's army, legal and education systems. This is how the cauliflower arrived in Nepal!

Preparation time: 1 hour
Serves: 6

INGREDIENTS

½ kg mutton with bones
4 cups cauliflower florets
1 cup fresh green peas
4 stalks fresh garlic shoots
1 ½ cups mustard oil
5 cloves
2 bay leaves
4 small cardamoms
1 big cardamoms
2 small sticks cinnamon
¼ tsp. fenugreek seeds
3 tsp. garlic paste
2 tsp. ginger paste
½ tsp. turmeric powder
1 tsp. coriander powder
1 tsp. cumin powder
1 tsp. red chilli powder
Salt to taste

PREPARATION

In Nepal, mutton is always consumed with the fat, skin and bones, however you can remove the fat and skin to suit your taste, since it is definitely a healthier option.

Heat 1 cup mustard oil in a pressure cooker till it smokes, add the fenugreek seeds, let them splutter and turn black, then add the whole spices, bay leaves, cloves, small and big cardamoms and cinnamon sticks. Add the meat, salt and ¼ tsp. turmeric powder, stir for 2 minutes until the meat turns to a dark colour, add the ginger garlic paste and stir for 2 minutes. Add the dry spices, coriander, cumin and red chilli powder, mix well and cook till oil separates. Pressure cook for 3 whistles. Cut the cauliflower into medium-sized florets, slice the stem in half without cutting through. In a wok heat ½ cup of oil till it smokes, add the cauliflower, add ¼ tsp. turmeric powder and salt. Stir and cover and cook till the cauliflower is half-cooked. Once the mutton is cooked open the pressure cooker and add the mutton gravy to the cauliflower and gently mix the two together. Add the peas and salt to taste, stir till the ingredients are well cooked but maintain their shape. Just before serving add the green garlic shoots, stir for a minute and serve piping hot.

Khasi Ko Masu

Kwati Chara Tare Ko

*Masu Koche
Ko Parwal*

Kwati Chara Tare Ko

Fried Mixed Sprouted Beans and Chicken

Kwati is a combination of nine types of beans, mainly cow peas, black-eyed peas, black lentils, chickpeas, soya beans, kidney beans, fava beans, green beans and field peas, all very nutritious and full of protein. You can use as many as available.

Preparation time: 45 minutes
Serves: 6

INGREDIENTS

½ kg boneless chicken
4 cups kwati
⅔ cup mustard oil
⅔ cup chopped onions
8 garlic cloves cut lengthways
2 bay leaves
½ tsp. fenugreek seeds
½ tsp. cumin seeds
1 tsp. carom seeds
2 tbsp. ground onion paste
1 tbsp. garlic paste
1 tbsp. ginger paste
¼ tsp. timur powder
1 ½ tsp. red chilli powder
1 ½ tsp. coriander powder
2 tsp. cumin powder
1 tsp. turmeric powder
1 ½ cup chopped tomatoes
Salt to taste

PREPARATION

Sprouting beans at home: Soak the beans in water for half an hour, drain the water and wrap in a moist muslin cloth and keep in a dark place. Next day, wash the beans and repeat the process, do this for 3-4 days till they sprout. Wash thoroughly to avoid a musty smell. You can buy sprouted beans as well.

Cut the chicken in 1 inch pieces, marinate in salt and a pinch of turmeric for 30 minutes. Heat the mustard oil till it smokes, then add the fenugreek, cumin, carom seeds and bay leaves. When the seeds darken add the chopped garlic and onions and stir till the onions are golden in colour. Put in the chicken pieces and stir for 3 minutes, remove the chicken and keep aside. To the same oil add the sprouts and stir till well coated with the oil. Add salt and turmeric powder, keep stirring till half-cooked, now add the chicken and on medium heat cover and cook, keep stirring from time to time till both are nearly cooked. In a bowl combine the onion, garlic, ginger pastes, chopped tomatoes, spices and mix well. Add to the pan and cook till the oil separates, stirring to incorporate all the ingredients together. Make sure the chicken and the beans are well cooked, if needed, add ½ cup of water and cover till cooked. This dish is a dry preparation and is a great accompaniment to rice or beaten rice.

Masu Koche Ko Parwal

Pointed Gourd Stuffed with Minced Chicken

Cottage cheese or potatoes can be used as a vegetarian option.

Preparation time: 30 minutes
Serves: 6

INGREDIENTS

10 parwals
¼ cup mustard oil
½ cup vegetable oil for frying
½ kg minced chicken
1 large onion, sliced
½ cup finely chopped spring onions
¼ tsp. asafoetida
1 tbsp. garlic paste
½ cup grated cheese/cream cheese
1 tsp. cumin powder
½ tsp. timur powder
Salt to taste

PREPARATION

Scrape the skin off the *parwals* and cut off one tip. With the help of a small, thin knife and teaspoon, scoop the seeds out of the gourds and make them hollow. Steam for 15 minutes and put into a bowl of cold water with a few ice cubes to retain their green colour. Heat a wok and add the mustard oil and heat till it smokes, add the sliced onions and sauté till translucent. Add the minced chicken and cover and cook till it changes colour to a light brown, keep stirring while cooking. Add the garlic paste, cumin and *timur* powder and stir for 2 minutes. Lower the heat, then add the cheese, spring onions and salt. Stir till the cheese melts and take off the fire. The cheese adds taste and moisture to the chicken mixture, but can be avoided if you want. Dry the *parwals* with a muslin cloth then stuff each well with the chicken mixture. Heat the vegetable oil in a pan and shallow fry on all sides.

Aaloo Chukauni

Potato and Yogurt Salad

This tasty potato dish hails from Palpa district in Nepal and can be served like a salad during summer. It is eaten as an accompaniment with sel roti or baras.

Preparation time: 20 minutes
Serves: 6

INGREDIENTS

4 medium-sized potatoes
2 red chillies
4 green chillies
¼ tsp. fenugreek seeds
2 ½ cups yogurt
1 medium-sized onion
½ tsp. turmeric powder
¼ tsp. timur powder
2 tbsp. mustard oil
Salt to taste

PREPARATION

Boil the potatoes, skin and cut into cubes, slice the onions. Heat the red and green chillies over an open flame till they are seared black and then grind them. Whisk the yogurt till smooth and add all the ingredients except the oil and fenugreek seeds, mix gently. Heat the mustard oil till it smokes, then add the fenugreek seeds, let them turn dark, then pour over the yogurt, mix and serve.

Aaloo Pyaj Ko Ras

Potato and Onion Soup

Preparation time: 30 minutes
Serves: 6

INGREDIENTS

2 ½ cups chopped potatoes
2 cups onions
½ cup green peas
1 tomato (optional)
½ cup green onions (optional)
½ cup ghee
¼ tsp. asafoetida
¼ tsp. fenugreek seeds
1 tsp. cumin seeds
½ tsp. turmeric powder
1 tbsp. garlic paste
1 tbsp. ginger paste
3 slit green chillies
Salt to taste

PREPARATION

Chop the potatoes into 1 inch cubes, quarter the onions in the same size. Heat the *ghee* in a wok and add the fenugreek seeds and cook to a brown colour, splutter the cumin and asafoetida, then add the potatoes; stir and cover and cook till the potatoes change colour. Add the salt and turmeric powder and cover and cook on medium heat for 2 minutes. Add the garlic, ginger paste and slit green chillies, cover and cook again for another 2 minutes. Add the tomatoes and green peas, mix with the potatoes then add 3 cups of water and let the mixture come to a boil. Add chopped green onions and cook for a minute. Garnish with chopped green coriander.

Aaloo Chuk

Aaloo Bakula

Aaloo
Chukauni

Aaloo Pyaj
Ko Ras

Aaloo Bakula

Potatoes and Broad Beans

Preparation time: 20 minutes
Serves: 6

INGREDIENTS

2 cups bakula
1 ½ cups cubed potatoes
½ cup oil
1 ½ tsp. cumin seeds
½ tsp. fenugreek seeds
½ tsp. turmeric powder
1 tsp. coriander powder
1 ½ tsp. cumin powder
1 tsp. chilli powder
2 tbsp. onion paste
1 tbsp. ginger paste
1 tbsp. garlic paste
1 ½ cup chopped tomatoes
Salt to taste

PREPARATION

Deseed the *bakula* beans, retain some tender skins and chop them into 1 inch pieces. Chop the potatoes to the same size and keep aside. Heat oil in a heavy-bottomed pan and splutter the fenugreek and cumin seeds, cook till they change colour and add the potatoes and beans. Stir till the potatoes are golden, then add the onion, garlic and ginger paste and stir for 2 minutes. Add the dry spices and salt and cover and cook till well integrated. Add the tomatoes and cook on low heat for another 5 minutes. Once the potatoes and beans are tender, add ½ cup of water, if necessary. You can dry out the liquid and serve dry or as a gravy.

Aaloo Chuk

Potatoes with Concentrated Lemon Juice

Preparation time: 30 minutes
Serves: 4

INGREDIENTS

½ kg small potatoes
½ cup mustard oil/ghee
6 red chillies halved
½ tsp. cumin
½ tsp. fenugreek seeds
½ tsp. turmeric powder
1 tsp. red chilli powder
1 tsp. cumin powder
1/4 tsp. timur powder
1 tbsp. ginger
2 tbsp. chuk amilo (lemon concentrate)
Salt to taste

PREPARATION

Wash the potatoes well and retain the skin, cut in half and parboil with a pinch of salt. Drain and keep aside. Heat oil till it smokes, add the chilli, fenugreek and cumin seeds and cook till they splutter and change colour. Add the potatoes and sprinkle the salt and turmeric powder on top, now mix and keep stirring till the potatoes turn crisp and golden. Mix the ginger paste, red chilli and cumin powder in ¼ cup of water, pour over the potatoes and keep stirring till crisp and golden. If necessary, add 1 tbsp. oil to make the potatoes crispy. Add the *timur* powder and *chuk amilo*, the potatoes should change colour to a dark brown. Garnish with chopped coriander and serve hot.

33

Paani Roti

Wheat Bread in Lentil Soup

This nourishing dish is a meal in itself, including whole wheat rotis, lentils and vegetables cooked together on slow heat and garnished with a nice dollop of sizzling ghee, usually eaten after a long day of fasting.

Preparation time: 45 minutes
Serves: 6

INGREDIENTS

1 ½ cups kerau ko daal (green split peas/chana daal)
2 cups potatoes cut in cubes
2 cups spinach or green zucchini shoots
2 whole red chillies
2 bay leaves
1 tsp. cumin seeds
2 tbsp. coarsely ground ginger
1 ½ tsp. red chilli powder
1 tsp. turmeric powder
2 tbsp. coriander powder
2 tbsp. cumin powder
½ cup ghee/oil

ROTI

1 ½ cups whole wheat flour
½ cup water

PREPARATION

Wash the *daal* and soak in water for half an hour. Add 2 slices of ginger, ½ tsp. turmeric powder and salt to the *daal* with 3 cups of water and pressure cook for 3 whistles, keep aside. Slowly add water to the wheat flour to make a soft pliable dough. Roll out round *rotis,* not too thin or thick. First cut the rotis length ways into 2 inch strips, then diagonally to make diamond shapes, keep aside.

In a separate pan add *ghee*/oil and temper with whole red chillies, bay leaves and cumin seeds and let them splutter and turn brown. Then add chopped potatoes, salt and turmeric powder and stir till the potatoes are golden brown. Add crushed ginger and spices and stir for 2 minutes till the raw smell dissipates. Add the cooked *daal* into the pan and mix with the potatoes, cook for 2 minutes. When the *daal* mixture is boiling, slowly add the diamond-shaped roti pieces and roughly chopped spinach. Cover until the pieces of *roti* are cooked, then add water to adjust to the right semi-liquid consistency. Serve with a generous serving of hot *ghee* and lemon wedges.

Iskus Tare Ko

Raayo Saag

Iskus Tare Ko

Fried Chayote Squash

Preparation time: 20 minutes
Serves: 6

INGREDIENTS

4 big squashes
Oil for deep-frying
1 tsp. cumin seeds
1 tsp. ginger paste
1 tsp. turmeric powder
1 tsp. cumin powder
4 green chillies, sliced lengthways
Salt to taste

PREPARATION

Wash and peel the squashes; slice lengthways into six pieces. Heat the oil in a wok and fry the sliced squashes till they change colour. Remove excess oil, just keeping approximately 1 tbsp. in the pan. Add the cumin seeds to the oil and let them splutter, add the ginger paste, cumin powder, turmeric powder and salt. Add the squash and stir till the raw smell of the spices dissipates and the squash is coated with the spices. Add sliced green chillies and stir for 2 minutes.

Raayo Saag

Mustard Greens

Preparation time: 20 minutes

Serves: 6

INGREDIENTS

2 bunches raayo saag (mustard greens)
2 tbsp. mustard oil
4 whole red chillis
½ tsp. fenugreek seeds
5 whole garlic cloves
1 tbsp. garlic paste
½ tbsp. ginger paste
Salt to taste

PREPARATION

Roughly chop the mustard greens, wash well and keep aside. Heat oil till it smokes. Add fenugreek seeds, red chillies and garlic cloves and cook till they turn colour. Add the chopped greens and sauté for 2 minutes. Add the crushed ginger garlic paste and salt, mix well and cook till the *saag* is cooked and water has dried. The mustard greens are best if prepared just before serving, retaining a crunch to the dish.

OPTION

Add 2 tbsp. of corn flour to the oil and sauté for a few minutes till it changes colour, then add the mustard greens and cook as above.

Aaloo Gajar Kerau Ko Achar

*Aaloo Bhaang
Ko Achar*

Bhaang Ko Achar

Mula Ko Achar

Haryo Lasun Sande Ko

Bhaang Ko Achar

Hemp Seed Pickle

Preparation time: 20 minutes
Serves: 8

INGREDIENTS

1 cup bhaang (hemp seeds)
1 tbsp. mustard oil
½ tsp. timur powder
1 tsp. red chilli powder
½ tsp. fenugreek seeds
1 tsp. chuk amilo (concentrate of lemon)
4 cloves sliced garlic
4 green chillies
2 red chillies
Salt to taste
½ cup water

PREPARATION

Dry roast the *bhaang* seeds in a pan for 2 minutes, cool and grind to a fine powder. Sear the red and green chillies on an open flame. Mix the dry ingredients in a bowl, add the water and *chuk amilo* and stir into a thick paste. Heat the oil till it smokes, add the fenugreek seeds and fry till they turn black, add the garlic cloves and fry to a golden colour, pour into the *bhaang* mixture. You can keep this mixture in the fridge for up to a week.

AALOO ACHAR WITH BHAANG
Boil 4 potatoes and cut into cubes, add the prepared *bhaang achar,* adjust the seasoning and consistency according to your liking, mix and serve.

Aaloo Gajar Kerau Ko Achar

Potato, Carrot and Fresh Peas Pickle

Preparation time: 20 minutes

Serves: 6

INGREDIENTS

2 cups boiled potatoes
2 cups chopped carrots
½ cup fresh green peas
½ cup chopped onions
1 tsp. julienned ginger
¼ cup chopped spring onions
3 garlic cloves, sliced lengthways
3 chopped green chillies
¼ cup lemon juice
1 tsp. red chilli powder
¼ tsp. timur powder
Salt to taste
2 tbsp. mustard oil
¼ tsp. fenugreek seeds

PREPARATION

Chop the boiled potatoes, carrots and onions into ½ inch cubes. Place all the ingredients except the mustard oil and fenugreek seeds in a bowl and mix well. Heat the oil in a small wok till it smokes, add the fenugreek seeds and fry till they are black, add to the bowl and mix.

38

Haryo Lasun Sande Ko

Tempered Green Garlic Shoots

Preparation time: 20 minutes
Serves: 6

INGREDIENTS

20 green garlic shoots
4 pieces sliced ginger
4 cloves garlic
2 red chillies
1 tsp. timur
3 tbsp. sesame seed powder
3 tbsp. mustard oil
2 tbsp. lemon juice
Salt to taste

PREPARATION

Wash the garlic shoots well, cut into 2 inch pieces and pat dry. Broil on charcoal or an open gas flame till they are cooked and charred. Remove the black skin and keep aside. Charcoal-grill the ginger, garlic and chillies till they are charred, then place in a mortar and pestle, add salt and the *timur* seeds, coarsely grind all these ingredients and add to the garlic shoots. Heat the mustard oil till it smokes and add to the mixture, add lemon juice and mix all the ingredients and serve.

Haryo Lasun Dahi Hale Ko

Green Garlic Shoots in Yogurt

Preparation time: 20 minutes
Serves: 6

INGREDIENTS

4 cups chopped green garlic shoots/green onions
4 cups yogurt
½ tsp. timur
1 tsp. red chilli powder
1 tsp. roasted cumin powder
¼ tsp. turmeric powder
2 tbsp. mustard oil
1 tbsp. sliced garlic
¼ tsp. fenugreek seeds
Salt to taste

PREPARATION

Like the previous recipe, charcoal broil and chop the garlic shoots in 1 inch pieces and keep aside. In a bowl add the yogurt, cumin, red chilli powder, *timur* and salt and whisk till smooth; add the garlic shoots and mix gently. Heat the mustard oil till it smokes and add the fenugreek seeds till they splutter and turn dark, add the sliced garlic and cook till golden brown, take the oil off the flame and add the turmeric powder, swirl and add to the yogurt mixture. Serve as an accompaniment to a typical Nepali *daal bhaat* meal.

Makai Ko Kheer

Gud Bhuja

Makai Ko Kheer

Fresh Corn Pudding

Preparation time: 30 minutes
Serves: 6

INGREDIENTS

2 cups fresh tender kernel corn
1 cup ghee
1 cup sugar
2 cups milk
1 tbsp. small cardamom powder
1 pinch black pepper

PREPARATION

Roughly crush the corn kernels, heat the *ghee* in a pressure cooker, add the corn and stir for 2 minutes till well coated with the *ghee.* Add the sugar and keep stirring till it melts, add the milk, mix and pressure cook for 3 whistles. After 1 whistle reduce to medium heat. Open the pressure cooker and check the consistency of the corn pudding, it should be semi-solid. Add the cardamom and pepper powder and mix well. This pudding should be served hot.

Gud Bhuja

Rice with Molasses

Preparation time: 20 minutes
Serves: 6

INGREDIENTS

2 tbsp. ghee
1 cup molasses/sugar
3 cups cooked rice
½ cup dry fruits (optional)

PREPARATION

Heat a pan and add the *ghee,* add the molasses and stir till it melts, lower the heat and add the cooked rice. Gently fold in the rice and mix it with the molasses. Once the rice and molasses are integrated, you can garnish with chopped dry fruits.

TAMANG

The Tamang community originates from the high hills of Nepal, mainly in the Ramechap valley and the Sinduli hills, around the Kathmandu valley. The name Tamang means horse trader and they form the largest group of Tibeto-Burman speaking people of the Himalayan region. They have their own unique language as well as lifestyle: 90 per cent of the community follow Buddhism, with a smattering of Hindu and Jhankari beliefs. The Lamas of this community are trained in Lamaistic Buddhist rituals and procedures, which are performed during religious ceremonies, weddings and funerals. The Tamangs are very skilled in the art of weaving of sheep wool jackets in the old traditional ways. They are also carpenters, masons and the Buddhist priests are trained in the fine art of Thangka (Buddhist scroll) paintings. They celebrate a blend of Buddhist and Hindu festivals of Sonam Lhosar, Temal and Dassain.

At high altitudes, their staple crops are maize, barley, wheat, millet and potato. They grow rice as well at lower altitudes. Their main food is *dhindo* (maize porridge), *batuk* (black lentil fritters), yams, fermented greens, meat and dried meat.

The traditional Lepcha flower 'Totola' or 'Ko Ko Medo' in Tamang and 'Pasang Meto' in Sherpa, is used for special ceremonies such as births, weddings, worship and funerals. It is also said to have medicinal properties.

Buff Sukuti Ko Ledo

Dried Buffalo Meat Gravy

Smoked or dried meat is a delicacy in Nepal and widely consumed by all communities from the north to the south. The practice of smoking meat was prevalent due to the lack of fresh meat during the winter season in the past. In spite of the availability of meat throughout the year now, due to ease in communication, this tasty dish is still extremely popular.

Preparation time: 30 minutes
Serves: 4

INGREDIENTS

½ kg buffalo sukuti
¼ cup mustard oil
1 cup chopped onions
1 cup chopped tomatoes
1 tbsp. coarsely ground garlic
1 tbsp. coarsely ground ginger
1 tsp. coriander powder
1 tsp. cumin powder
½ tsp. red chilli powder
½ tsp. turmeric powder
Salt to taste

PREPARATION

Heat the oil, add the chopped onions and fry till translucent, add the ginger, garlic and stir for another 2 minutes. Then add the dry spices, tomatoes and salt, cook till oil separates then add the *sukuti* pieces and mix with the other ingredients till well integrated. Add 2 cups of water and cook covered on medium heat till the meat is cooked. Traditionally, the meat remains tough but cook according to personal preference; add water if necessary to make a gravy. This dish can be eaten with rice, *dhindo*, or *batuk*.

Batuk

*Phapar
Ko Phulaura*

*Buff Sukuti
Ko Ledo*

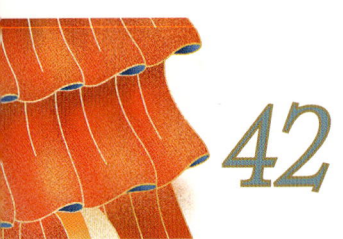

Batuk

Fried Black Lentil Doughnuts

*These fried lentil doughnuts are common to many communities but are
a must for celebrations in the Tamang and Magar communities, during
the Sonam Lhosar, Tamang New Year and Magar Maghe festivals.
The celebration is not complete without this delicacy.*

Preparation time: 30 minutes
Serves: 8

INGREDIENTS

2 cups black bean lentils
1 tbsp. ginger juice
Salt to taste
1 tsp. asafoetida
Oil for deep-frying

PREPARATION

Soak the lentils overnight. While washing the black lentils,
retain half the black skin, grind to a coarse paste. Mix all
the ingredients and whisk well for 5 minutes, then keep
aside to rest for 30 minutes. Heat the oil and take 1 tbsp.
of batter in your oiled palm, make a hole in the centre and
slide into the oil; deep-fry both sides to a golden brown.

Phapar Ko Phulaura

Buckwheat Fluffy Balls

Preparation time: 30 minutes
Serves: 8

INGREDIENTS

2 cups buckwheat flour
1 tsp. red chilli powder
1 tbsp. ginger juice
1 tbsp. chopped green chillies
1 tbsp. chopped green coriander
Salt to taste
Oil for deep-frying

PREPARATION

Mix the flour with enough water to make a thick paste, add all the ingredients and keep aside to rest for 1 hour. Heat oil and drop in 1 tbsp. of the batter in the shape of a ball into the hot oil and fry on medium heat till they fluff up and cook on the inside. Serve piping hot.

MAGAR

The Magar community is one of the oldest known indigenous tribes of Nepal, mainly concentrated in the mid-Himalayas, living around the foothills of the Dhaulagiri mountain to the west of the Gandaki river, but due to eastward migration they have spread all over Nepal. The original home of the Magars was called Magarant. Having lived in very close proximity with the Khas and Brahman tribes of Nepal, they have adopted many of their religious and cultural beliefs. They practise Bon Buddhism, Hinduism and Shamanism. Their integration into the Hindu religion is evident from the fact that the head priest in the main temple in Gorkha is a Magar. They celebrate the festivals of Dassain, Tihar and Maghe Sankaranti.

Their main occupation was agriculture, carpentry, stone quarrying and masonry work. They are famous to date as the largest ethnic group to have joined the military forces from the time of King Prithvi Bir Bikram Shah Dev, the Thakuri King of Gorkha, who is famous for the unification of Nepal. They are still a dominant force in the Nepal army with the Purano Gorakh battalion consisting only of Magar soldiers. Many from their community joined the Indian and British armies as well and have been able to raise the standard of living of their families and community with the remittance earned from their soldiering.

The Magar community have been self-sufficient with their terrace farming in the mountain areas, growing corn, millet and buckwheat, migrating to more arable lands around the rivers more suitable to growing rice, fruit and vegetables.

The traditional food of the Magars like other ethnic communities, is also *dhindo* (maize porridge), *batuk* (fried lentil doughnuts), *phulaura* (fried lentil balls), *tarul* (yam), sukuti (dried meat) and pork preparations accompanied with *gundruk* (fermented greens). Their meal is not complete without copious amounts of home-brewed *kodo ko raksi*, a local alcoholic drink made out of millet.

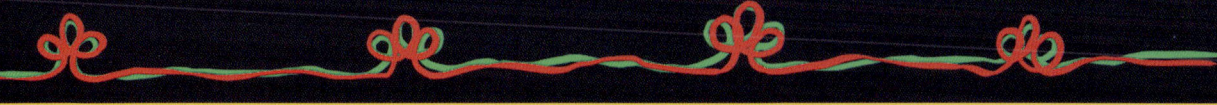

Sutkeri
Kukhura Ko Jhol

Tarul Tare Ko

Makai Ko Dhindo

Makai Ko Dhindo

Maize Porridge

Preparation time: 15 minutes
Serves: 4

INGREDIENTS

5 cups water
2 cups maize flour
1 tbsp. ghee

PREPARATION

Heat the water in a heavy-bottomed pan till it boils, add the maize flour, lower the heat and mix vigorously with a wooden spatula till well integrated into a porridge consistency. Serve hot, make a dent in the middle with the back of the spatula and pour a tablespoon of hot *ghee* in the centre.

45

Tarul Tare Ko

Fried Yam

Preparation time: 20 minutes
Serves: 6

INGREDIENTS

½ kg tarul (yam)
1 tbsp. oil
½ tsp. cumin seeds
½ tsp. turmeric powder
1 tsp. red chilli powder
Salt to taste

PREPARATION

Boil the *tarul* until it cooks; skin and slice into ½ inch round pieces. Heat oil and splutter the cumin seeds till they change colour, add the yam pieces and stir gently, coating them with the oil. Add the dry spices and cook for a further 5 minutes on mild heat. Garnish with chopped coriander and serve.

Sutkeri Kukhura Ko Jhol

Local Chicken Curry for Nursing Mothers

This chicken curry is cooked specially for nursing mothers during the lactation period (sutkeri) but can be enjoyed by all due to its delicious taste.

Preparation time: 30 minutes

Serves: 8

INGREDIENTS

1 kg local chicken
1 tbsp. mustard oil
2 tbsp. ghee
2 bay leaves
½ cup sliced onions
2 tbsp. rice
½ cup chopped tomatoes
1 tbsp. coarsely ground ginger
1 tbsp. coarsely ground garlic
2 tsp. garam masala powder
(small and large cardamom, cinnamon,
cloves, black pepper, mace and nutmeg)
1 tsp. turmeric powder
2 tsp. cumin powder
1 tsp. coriander powder
1 tsp. chilli powder
2 tsp. carom seeds
Salt to taste

PREPARATION

Cut the chicken into 2 inch pieces, wash and keep aside. In a pan, dry roast the rice grains till they change colour lightly, cool and grind. Heat the oil in a heavy-bottomed pan or pressure cooker and add the mustard oil, heat till it smokes and add the bay leaves and sliced onions. Cook until the onions change colour and add the chicken and stir till well coated with the oil, add the turmeric powder and salt and cook for another 2 minutes. Now add the ginger garlic paste, chopped tomatoes, rice powder, dry spices and stir until well integrated and the oil separates. Add 2 cups of water and cook on medium heat for 20 minutes (2 whistles in a pressure cooker) till the chicken is cooked. Once the chicken is cooked add water to make the consistency of the gravy according to your preference. Before serving, heat the *ghee* in a small pan and add the carom seeds, let them splutter and pour on top of the chicken curry, mix and serve.

GURUNG

The Gurung community, traditionally, is a Sino-Tibetan tribe that entered Nepal via Mustang from Tibet during the seventh century. They inhabited the southern slopes of the Annapurna range in Central Nepal in the Gandaki province. They have settled in Manang, Mustang, Lamjung and Kaski, Parbat, Dolpo, Syangja and Dhading districts.

They are animistic in their traditions and follow Bon and Buddhist religions with Shamanistic elements. These hardy hill people make extremely professional soldiers and were recruited in King Prithvi Narayan Shah's army during the unification of Nepal. They still enjoy their martial status and join the British and Indian Gurkhas. To date, the Nepali Army has a battalion named Kaali Bahadur, which recruits soldiers only from the Gurung community.

The Gurungs grow rice, wheat, maize, millet and potatoes and rear sheep as a source of meat and wool. They celebrate Tamu Lhosar and Dassain as their main festivals and have *Rodi Ghar* (singing) and *Sorathi (*dancing) traditions, which are famous in Nepal. Their main meal consists of rice or *dhindo* made out of millet or buckwheat flour, accompanied with *sukuti* (dried buffalo meat), lentils, *gundruk* (fermented greens) in a curry or pickle form and *sinki* (radish tap roots). They consume sheep, goat and chicken and a variety of vegetables grown in their region.

*Gundruk Aaloo
Bodi Tare Ko*

Bodi Ko Biraula

Kukhura Ko Masu Ko Achar

Latte

Latte

Sweet Sticky Rice

This sweet sticky rice is usually prepared during the New Year festival of Tamu Lhosar, which falls around the end of December every year. A special variety of rice called Anadi, which is glutinous, is used for the preparation.

Preparation time: 30 minutes
Serves: 6

INGREDIENTS

2 cups latte rice
½ cup ghee
1 ¼ cups molasses or 1 ½ cups sugar
6 cloves
8 small cardamoms
1 bay leaf

PREPARATION

Soak the rice in 2 cups of water for an hour. Heat *ghee* and add the bay leaf, cloves and roughly pounded cardamom. Add the rice and stir till all ingredients are combined well, keep stirring on low heat till rice is well coated with the *ghee* and starts sticking to the pan. Add the crumbled molasses and stir again till it is melted and integrated with the rice. Add ½ cup hot water and mix well. Add 1 ½ cups hot water and stir, pressure cook on low heat for 2 whistles. Remove from heat and serve hot.

Kukhura Ko Masu Ko Achar

Chicken Pickle

This dish was a favourite during long journeys in the old days, since no water is used in its preparation and so it lasted for days without refrigeration.

Preparation time: 30 minutes

Serves: 6

INGREDIENTS

½ kg boneless chicken cubes
½ cup mustard oil
1 tsp. fenugreek
4 whole chillies
1 tbsp. garlic paste
1 tbsp. ginger paste
½ tsp. turmeric powder
1 tbsp. coriander powder
1 tbsp. cumin powder
1 tbsp. red chilli powder
3 tsp. sesame powder
2 tbsp. lemon juice
Salt to taste

PREPARATION

Cut chicken breast into 2 inch cubes, heat oil in a heavy-bottomed pan and add the fenugreek seeds. Cook till the seeds turn black, then add the chillies and chicken cubes, cook till the chicken changes colour and is cooked. Add turmeric powder and salt and stir for 2 minutes, then add the garlic ginger paste and dry spices, keep stirring till well integrated with the chicken. Add the lemon juice and sesame powder and stir again for 2 minutes.

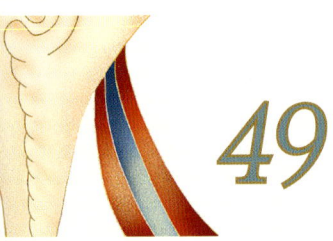

Bodi Ko Biraula

Black-Eyed Beans

Preparation time: 30 minutes
Serves: 6

INGREDIENTS

2 cups bodi (black-eyed beans)
½ cup mustard oil
½ tsp. fenugreek seeds
1 tbsp. garlic paste
1 tbsp. ginger paste
1 ¼ tsp. cumin powder
1 ¼ tsp. coriander powder
½ tsp. turmeric powder
1 tsp. chilli powder
Salt to taste

PREPARATION

Rinse the beans well and soak overnight in water. Boil in a pressure cooker with 2 cups of water, salt and ½ tsp. turmeric powder for 1 whistle, strain the water and keep aside. Heat the mustard oil in a heavy-bottomed wok and temper the fenugreek seeds till they turn black, add the ginger garlic paste and stir till it changes colour. Add the dry spices as well and stir again for 2 minutes then add the boiled beans and mix gently till all the spices are well integrated with the beans. Add salt and cook for another 5 minutes on low heat. Serve hot.

Gundruk Aaloo Bodi Tare Ko

Fried Fermented Dried Greens, Potatoes and Soya Beans

Preparation time: 45 minutes
Serves: 6

INGREDIENTS

1 cup potatoes
1 cup gundruk (fermented dried greens)
1 cup bhatmas (dried soya beans)
1 tbsp. finely chopped green chillies
1 ½ tsp. red chilli powder
½ cup finely chopped onions
2 tbsp. lemon juice
Salt to taste
2 tbsp. chopped coriander leaves

PREPARATION

Soak the beans in water overnight, drain, deep-fry and keep aside. Cut potatoes into thin sticks and deep-fry to a golden brown colour. Chop the *gundruk* finely and fry, mix all the ingredients and toss well. Serve hot.

Spices

Spices are the elixir that adds flavour to food and life, stimulating the taste buds and scintillating our senses to another level. They not only enhance flavour but have a myriad medicinal attributes as well; their consumption aids digestion and provides nutrition.

Spices are obtained from plants; their use and potency are determined by the part of the plant that is in play, mainly roots, seeds, stems, leaves, buds, flowers, fruits and barks. Spices have been in existence as an integral part of culinary tradition since time immemorial, forging trade routes and discovery of new lands, rejuvenating the living and embalming the dead. Each spice has its own unique flavour, singly or in combination, elevating the taste of any dish to extraordinary levels.

Toasting spices brings out their flavour to the maximum, while grinding them releases essential oils, which enhances the dishes they are added to with fragrance and taste. Tempering is another form of cooking that infuses the taste of the spice in the food and provides a burst of flavour. Spices vary from mild, hot to aromatic and are always more potent if used fresh as compared to dried and powdered. The stage of cooking that incorporates spices also holds import since whole spices like cinnamon, cardamom, cloves and bay leaves, seeds like cumin and fenugreek, are always tempered in hot oil at the very beginning of a preparation to infuse the oil with their aroma while the ground powder of these very same spices is added towards the end of cooking a dish in order to enable the aroma of these spices to stay in the dish, and atmosphere, heightening the awareness that something good is cooking.

Nepal is a country with the most diverse climate and topography, naturally producing a vast variety of spices which vibrantly flavour the local cuisine but were contained in their own regions due to lack of transportation. This treasure trove of spices have now exploded into the global arena and are easily available in the market, spicing and layering local and foreign cuisine with culinary nuances that are unique in flavour.

Spices in the Nepalese ethnic communities are used sparingly, just enough to bring out the flavour of the meat or vegetable to the optimum. The use of *jimbu* and *timur* to spice the dishes provide a burst of flavour that makes Nepali cuisine distinctly unique, creating its very own culinary masterpieces.

Weights and Measurements of Dry Ingredients

1 tsp. (teaspoon)	5 grams
1 tbsp. (tablespoon)	15 grams
¼ cup	50 grams
½ cup	115 grams
⅔ cup	150 grams
¾ cup	170 grams
1 cup	200 grams

A Few Tips on Nepali Cooking

Daal bhaat tarkari (lentils, rice and vegetables) is the trinity of Nepali classic food, which transports everyone to a happy and contented zone, guaranteeing a full stomach and a smile on the face. When *masu* (meat) and *achar* (pickle) are added, the satiation level knows no bounds!

Dhindo (porridge) made out of maize, millet or buckwheat, eaten with meat and vegetables is another favourite.

The traditional ways of cooking are *jhanne* (tempering), *bhutne* (stir frying), *tarne* (frying), *bapahune* (boiling) and *sandne* (marinating). Smoking, drying and fermenting meat and vegetables are other typical ways of preparing food.

Cooking with spices enhances the flavours of the dish and takes it to the next level. Nepalese cuisine is very lightly flavoured by spices, ensuring the taste of the meat and vegetables is brought out to the maximum.

Familiar spices used in Nepali cuisine are similar to Indian and other spices in Asia, therefore easily available in Asian stores worldwide. The spices which are typically Nepali are *timur* (sichuan pepper) and *jimbu* (Himalayan allium). The spices used by the Thakali, Sherpa and Rai Limbu communities like *jadi buti (marju/paan septi),* resembling fennel seeds and *chimping* (Nepali hogweed) and *philunge* (niger seeds) are rare and available mainly in the region or in specialty stores in Kathmandu. The use of chillies in the recipes can be reduced or increased according to personal taste.

Traditionally, meals are eaten with the right hand, using just the fingertips, pushing the food into the mouth with the thumb. It is scientifically proven that eating with the hands tantalizes the taste buds, improves digestion, regulates blood flow as well as helps manage food portions. Many believe in the profound emotional and spiritual connection with the food eaten with the hands. Happy finger-licking!

‘I don't measure a thing when I cook . . .
I just sprinkle and add stuff until I hear
the spirit of my ancestors' whisper
'That's enough, child'.
—A popular quote

Fermented Food

Fermenting food is a tradition that has been practised in Nepal since time immemorial and is popular to date. Awareness of the benefits of fermented food in gut health has made its ripples in the new culinary scenario. The mountainous regions of the country are covered in snow for the better part of the year and the unavailability of fresh food led to perfecting the art of smoking and fermenting. Thus, vegetables, grains and meats are dried, smoked and fermented for later use.

The reason for the consumption of fermented food in the fertile Kathmandu valley which abounds in the growth of fresh vegetables is an interesting one. King Prithvi Narayan Shah laid siege to the Kathmandu valley in 1768, for years trying to bring the Malla Kings to submission. During this blockade, the villagers being unable to grow fresh vegetables resorted to drying and fermenting radish and mustard leaves to eat in the cold winter months. This was the birth of *gundruk* and other fermented food as we know it today.

Studies in the field have proved that the fermentation of food promotes gut health. However, fermented food has a strong smell and flavour, which makes it an acquired taste. The main fermented vegetables are radish, mustard greens (*sinki, mula ko chana, gundruk*), a combination of lentils and yam stems (*masuara, titaura, bariya*) and fermented bamboo shoots (*tama*), soya bean (*kinema*) and wild lichens (*yangben*).

The art of drying and smoking meat is also popular in Nepal, the meat which is air-dried or smoked is called *sukuti* and is cooked on its own or with a combination of vegetables in a hot soup. The animals range from yak, buffalo and mutton to fish. In the old days, when hunting was prevalent, venison was also smoked for consumption later.

NEWAR

The Newari people have occupied the Kathmandu valley and its surrounding areas as its indigenous inhabitants since the seventh or eighth century. They spread slowly towards the eastern and western hills and Terai plains, mainly for business and trading purposes. This erudite society embodies the synthesis of Indo-Aryan descent as well as Tibeto-Burman ethnicities in a beautifully syncretic integration of art, culture, religion, language and cuisine. The Newars were predominantly Buddhist at the time of their inception, but after the coming of the Malla dynasty from the south during the eleventh century, Hinduism was well integrated into their religion and social practices. To date, they have effortlessly maintained a perfect balance and beautiful blend of both.

पर्वते बिग्रयो मोजले
नेवार बिग्रयो भोजले

'The Hill tribes of Nepal were ruined by their constant pursuit of enjoyment while the Newar people were ruined by their constant feasting!'

The Newars consistently rank as the most politically, economically and socially advanced community in Nepal. Their economic, social and religious practices are regulated by the *Gutthi* system, which constitutes a common trust, including arable and temple lands as assets. The Gutthis belong to the membership holders and all religious and social aspects are controlled by its governing body. This highly talented community boasts a large number of skilled artists, craftsmen, artisans and tradesmen. The Kathmandu Mandala resonates with the magic of their talent and expertise to date.

Food is an integral part of Newari culture and has developed over centuries, integrating and assimilating the various influences from the north and south.

Newari cuisine depicts its culture which consists of numerous religious festivals, all associated with copious amounts of feasting. Various food items are diligently prepared for different events, keeping the climate and nutrition in mind. Newari cuisine consists of the main staple, *ja* (rice), *cheura* (beaten rice), lentils, mainly buffalo meat, vegetables and pickles painstakingly prepared in various ways to please their palate and accommodate their pockets. The various Gutthis control and manage the fabric of society through the festivals and feasts, therefore, food is the crucial centripetal force of the Newari way of life.

Sama y Baji

Samay Baji is the auspicious food offered to the deities being worshipped at the beginning of any feast, ritual or celebration. This amalgamation of different food items signifies prosperity, good health, love, luck and happiness bestowed on the members partaking of this feast. In Newari culture, food preparation is considered to be a sacred art involving a blend of the five elements: earth, water, wind, fire and ether or space. These five elements are symbolized in the *samay baji,* which is offered to the gods before being consumed by the people as *prashad* (food blessed by the gods). It is a combination of carbohydrates, protein and fibre in the form of earth-signifying *cheura* (beaten rice), *Choeyla* (buffalo meat grilled and tempered with spices). Cooked *wo* or *bara* (lentil pancakes) and a boiled egg signify fire, and fried fish, water. Spinach, soya beans and ginger are all part of this feast. Locally brewed alcohol called *raksi* is also served as part of this sumptuous meal. After being beautifully decorated and offered to the deities, the food is consumed by the family and distributed to the community.

*Maas Daal
Ko Bara*

Wo Bara

Wo Bara

Green Gram Lentil Pancakes

Preparation time: 30 minutes
Serves: 4, Makes: 12

INGREDIENTS

2 ½ cups haryo mungi daal
(green gram lentil) with skin
1 tsp. garlic paste
2 tsp. ginger paste
½ tsp. cumin powder
½ tsp. asafoetida
Mustard oil for sautéing
Salt to taste

PREPARATION

Soak the mungi daal overnight or for at least 6 hours. Rinse the skin off and rub with your hands till the skin is removed, wash a couple of times till the *daal* is free of skin. Grind to a smooth paste and mix all the ingredients, except the oil, beat well to integrate and make the dough light and fluffy. Heat a griddle and spread a little oil on the surface. Take half a cup of paste in your hand and gently drop on the hot griddle, let it cook on medium heat for 1 minute then gently spread with your hand. It should be ¼ inch thickness, sprinkle little oil on top and when cooked, slowly flip to cook the other side. Drizzle oil on this side too and remove from the pan once cooked. Serve hot.

Maas Daal Ko Bara

Deep-Fried Black Gram Lentil Pancakes

Preparation time: 30 minutes
Serves: 4, Makes: 12

INGREDIENTS

2 ½ cups kaalo maas daal
(black gram lentils) with skin
1 finely chopped onion
½ cup chopped green coriander
2 tsp. ginger paste
1 tsp. garlic paste
½ tsp. cumin powder
½ tsp. asafoetida
Salt to taste
Oil for deep-frying

PREPARATION

Prepare the batter in the same way as the *Wo bara* and add all the ingredients except the oil, beat well till the batter is light and fluffy. Grease the palm of one hand with oil, take a spoon full of the batter in the palm of your hand, press down to make a circle of ¼ inch thickness, gently make a hole in the middle and slip into the hot oil. Deep-fry till golden brown on both sides. Serve hot with tomato or green coriander *achar*.

Chatamari

Rice Pancake with Minced Meat and Egg

Traditionally, buff minced meat was used for this recipe, but you can use any meat of your choice.

Preparation time: 30 minutes
Serves: 6
1 bara per person

INGREDIENTS

2 cups rice flour
2 cups water
Salt to taste

MINCED MEAT

6 eggs
250 grams buff/pork/mutton/chicken minced meat
2 tbsp. oil
1 tbsp. chopped garlic
2 tbsp. chopped onions
½ tsp. coriander powder
½ tsp. cumin powder
¼ tsp. turmeric powder
½ tsp. red chilli powder
Salt to taste

GARNISHING

¼ cup chopped onions
¼ cup tomatoes
1 tbsp. chopped green coriander
½ tsp. red chilli powder

PREPARATION

Heat a pan and add the garlic and onions to the pan, fry till translucent. Add minced meat and stir for 2 minutes. Add the spices and salt and cook till the meat changes colour, add 1 tbsp. water if necessary. When the meat is cooked, keep aside. Mix the rice flour and water to make a semi-liquid batter (pancake batter consistency). Heat a griddle and oil the surface, pour a ladle full of batter and spread gently to ½ inch thickness, cook for 1 minute. Sprinkle with cooked minced meat and gently break an egg on top of the meat mixture, add 1 tsp. oil around the *bara* and cover with a lid and cook for 3 minutes on low heat. Sprinkle salt and red chilli powder according to taste. The lentil pancake and egg need to cook through, add 1 tbsp. of oil on top of the pancake and gently flip over with the egg facing down. Add 1 tsp. of oil and cook for another 2 minutes and the *chatamari* is done. Mix the ingredients of the garnishing and keep aside. Serve with the egg side up sprinkled with the garnishing.

Haans Ko Choeyla

Barbecued Tempered Duck Meat

The Newars prefer buffalo meat to make this dish, but it tastes as good made with mutton or chicken, and best with duck.

Preparation time: 45 minutes
Serves: 6

INGREDIENTS

1 kg duck meat (should be 600 grams boneless)
1 ½ tsp. ginger juice and paste
1 tsp. garlic paste
½ tsp. fenugreek seeds
½ tsp. timur powder
1 tsp. cumin powder
1 tsp. red chilli powder
½ tsp. turmeric powder
½ cup chopped green garlic shoots
⅓ cup mustard oil
Salt to taste
1 tbsp. raw mustard oil
1 tbsp. water

PREPARATION

Debone the duck but retain the skin. Cut meat in ½ inch thick strips. The typical Newari-style *Choeyla* is Barbecued on hay. Please feel free to use coals if hay is unavailable. Barbecue the strips of meat till cooked, put the pieces of meat in a bowl and cut into 1 inch pieces, add all the ingredients except the raw oil and green garlic shoots. Wear gloves and mix all the ingredients well, squeezing the meat so the flavours seep in. Heat the mustard oil till it smokes and add to the bowl. Add the raw oil and water and green garlic shoots to the meat and mix again and serve. Tastes best accompanied with *cheura* (beaten rice).

Newari Street Food

Phokso Tare Ko

Batter Fried Lung

Preparation time: 45 minutes
Serves: 6

INGREDIENTS

1 kg mutton lung
250 grams maida (refined flour)
4 eggs
2 tsp. garlic paste
1 tsp. cumin powder
1 tsp. red chilli powder
Salt to taste
Mustard oil for frying

PREPARATION

Clean the lung and fit with a spout on one end. Make a batter with the *maida* flour and eggs, pour into the lung. Tie both ends of the lungs and boil in water for 30 minutes. Set aside to cool, then cut in 2 inch pieces. Heat a griddle and drizzle mustard oil, place a few pieces of the lung on it and cook both sides till it changes colour. Make a paste of the garlic, cumin, red chilli powder and salt, add the paste to the fried lungs and stir fry again till spices are cooked.

Shenlamu

Sautéed Liver

In Newari cuisine, the use of buffalo meat is prevalent, but you can use mutton or chicken liver instead.

Preparation time: 30 minutes
Serves: 6

INGREDIENTS

½ kg buffalo/mutton/chicken liver
2 tbsp. mustard oil
1 tsp. chilli powder
1 tsp. cumin powder
Salt to taste

PREPARATION

Parboil the liver in a cup of water with a pinch of salt, dry out on a kitchen towel and grill on a barbecue or preferably on charcoal fire. Remove and chop into 1 inch pieces. Add the dry spices and raw mustard oil, serve as snacks with *cheura* or with rice as part of a meal.

Parwal Tare Ko

Fried Pointed Gourd

Preparation time: 20 minutes
Serves: 6

INGREDIENTS

1 kg pointed gourd
1 tsp. cumin powder
1 tsp. red chilli powder
Oil for deep-frying
Salt to taste

PREPARATION

Wash the *parwal* well, scrape off the outer skin and cut both ends, slice in ¼ inch rounds and keep aside. Heat the oil and fry the pieces of pointed gourd till crisp. Remove oil from wok retaining 1 tbsp., add the gourd, cumin, red chilli powder and salt and stir fry for 2 minutes.

Kauli Tarkari

Tempered Cauliflower

Preparation time: 20 minutes
Serves: 6

INGREDIENTS

1 kg cauliflower
½ tsp. turmeric power
1 tbsp. coarsely ground garlic
1 tsp. cumin powder
¼ cup mustard oil
Salt to taste

PREPARATION

Break large cauliflower florets and keep aside, heat oil till it smokes and add the cauliflower, cover and cook on moderate heat till half-cooked, add ½ cup water, if necessary. Add the rest of the ingredients and sauté till cooked and the raw smell of the garlic and cumin disappears.

Saag Sande Ko

Tempered Spinach

Preparation time: 15 minutes
Serves: 4

INGREDIENTS

3 cups tender spinach leaves
½ cup roasted and coarsely ground soya bean
2 tsp. garlic paste
1 tsp. ginger paste
½ tsp. red chilli paste
1 tsp. cumin powder
Salt to taste
2 tbsp. raw mustard oil

PREPARATION

Wash the spinach leaves well, retain tender stems, blanch in hot water for 2 minutes and plunge into cold water to retain the colour. Dry roast the soya bean and grind coarsely. Add all the ingredients, including oil, mix gently and serve.

VARIATION

Using the same ingredients, one can replace the spinach with *bhatmas* (dry roasted soya beans), boiled eggs or thinly sliced *adua* (ginger). The soya beans have great nutritional value.

Yomari

Steamed Rice Dumplings Filled with Molasses

Preparation time: 45 minutes
Serves: 6

INGREDIENTS

2 cups rice flour
⅓ cup maida (refined flour)
2 tbsp. ghee
½ cup milk
½ cup warm water
1 tbsp. sesame seeds
2 cups molasses/concentrated milk
¼ cup chopped nuts optional
¼ cup grated coconut

PREPARATION

Heat water and milk in a pan and keep aside, place the rice flour and *maida* in a bowl and add 1 tbsp. *ghee* to it slowly add hot milky water to the flour and keep stirring to mix and form into a dough. When sufficiently cooled, knead into a soft pliable dough and keep aside. Heat even-sized pieces of molasses in a pan till they melt and form a thick sauce. Dry roast the sesame seeds, cool and grind and add to the molasses with the dry fruits and grated coconut. Grease your palm with oil. Form same-sized balls of the dough and take one in the palm of your hand and shape like a cylinder, roll and press one end to make a pointy tail, dip your thumb in a bowl of lukewarm water with 1 tbsp. of *ghee* in it. Make a hole with your thumb in the round end of the *yomari* and keep turning it slowly in your palm as the hole grows bigger. Fill the open end with the molasses sauce then slowly pinch the edges close and make two small ears on the other end. Place the *yomaris* in a steamer and cook for 20 minutes till light and fluffy.

VARIATION

Mix concentrated milk with dry fruits and coconut and stuff in the *yomari* instead of molasses. Best eaten hot!

161

Gwaramari

Deep-Fried Flour Balls

Preparation time: 20 minutes
Serves: 6-8

INGREDIENTS

2 cups refined flour
1 tsp. baking soda/powder
Salt to taste
Oil for deep-frying

PREPARATION

Mix the first three ingredients and make a thick paste, keep in a dry place for 4-5 hours. Whisk well, heat the oil in a frying pan and take a tbsp. of batter in your hand and drop into the hot oil. After it turns a golden colour, flip over to fry on the other side. The dent in the middle which comes from frying in a shallow pan makes it look like a *dumru* (drum). Serve hot with a cup of *masala* tea.

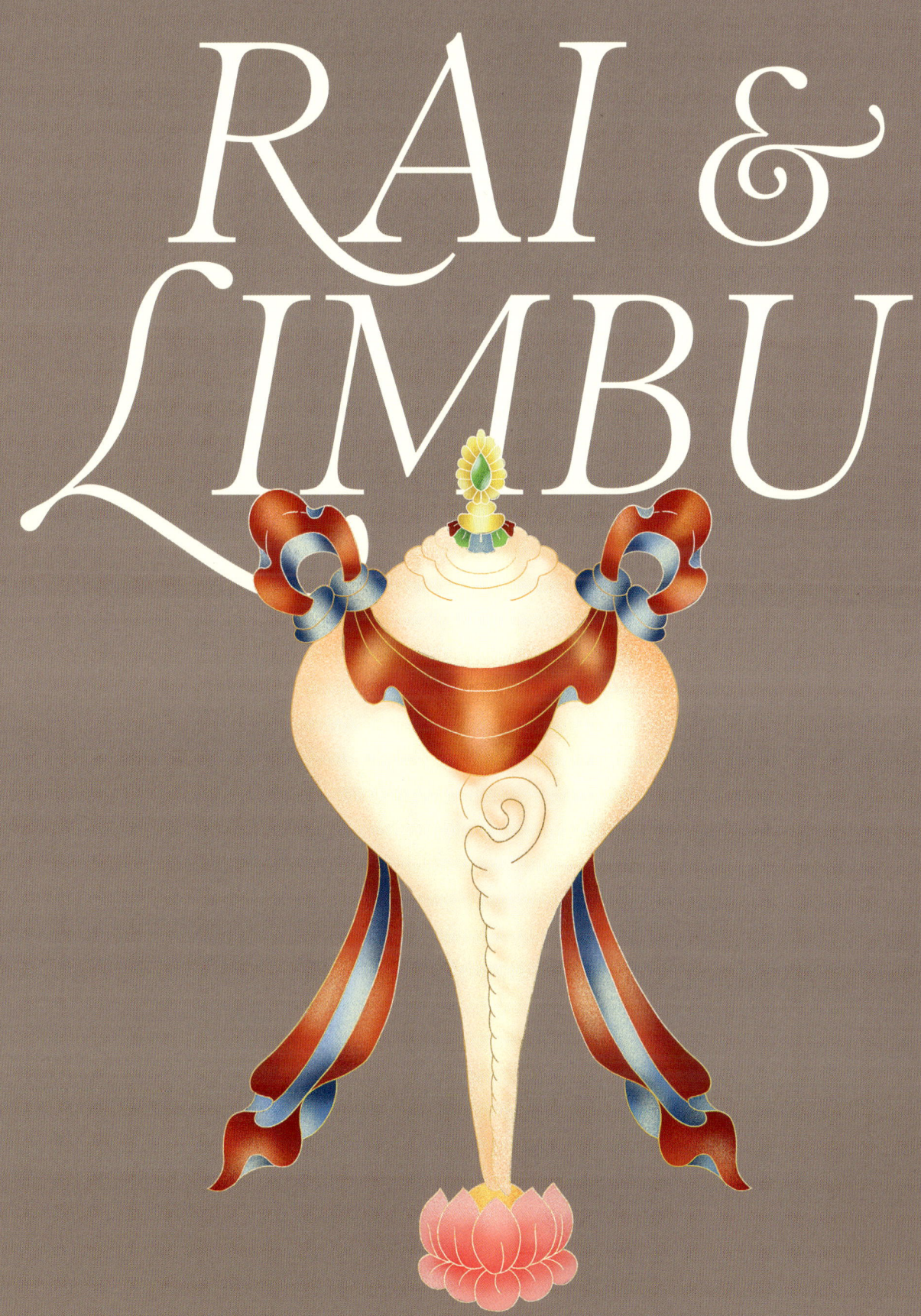

RAI &
LIMBU

The ethnic Kiratis are the indigenous inhabitants of eastern Nepal, and they are divided into two main groups.

Rai

The Rai people reside in the eastern Himalayan region of Nepal, in an area known as Manjh-Kirant (middle Kirant), which is basically the slopes of the Arun, Dudh Kosi, Sun Kosi and Tama Kosi rivers; they finally settled around the Bhote Kosi river.

Rais are renowned for their fearless martial nature and prowess and are therefore recruited into the British and Indian Gurkha battalions as well as the Nepali Army. Their religion is an integrated form of Lamaistic Buddhism and Hinduism emanating from animastic, nature and ancestor worship. The festivals of Bhumi Puja or Sakela, Nwagi and Wadangmi are celebrated by dancing and feasting with great gusto. On these occasions, they sacrifice chickens, pigs and buffaloes in honour of the gods, nature and themselves. Their main crops are wheat, maize, millet, mustard, rice, potatoes, beans and vegetables. In addition to these, they grow cotton, which together with sisal hemp is woven into colourful and durable material for their clothing.

Limbu

The Limbu or Yakhthung tribes are the second largest Sino-Tibetan tribe amongst the Kiratis hailing from Limbuwan or Pallo Kirat (far Kirat). Limbuwan includes the area east of the Arun river, extending all the way to the eastern border of Nepal, including the districts of Terathum, Sankhuwa Sabha, Dhankuta, Taplejung, Paanchthar, Morang, Sunsari, Jhapa and Ilam.

The Limbus cultivate rice, maize, wheat, millet and mustard for their consumption, the residue being utilized to make *raksi* and *tongba* (both local beers).

Apart from vegetables, they grow various fruits like guava, papaya, orange and banana. Buffaloes and cows are raised for milk, while goat, sheep and chicken are raised for meat.

The food of the Rai Limbu communities is similar to Nepali food, yet has its own ethnic connotations depending on the hilly region and the limited local produce. Boiled rice, *dhindo* (porridge), *sel roti* (rice flour doughnuts), *wachipa* (chicken meat with burnt chicken feathers, offals and rice), *kinema* (fermented soya bean), *sargemba* (pig's blood sausage), *yaangmaen-faaksa* (pork curry with wild lichens) and *philunge ko achar* (niger seed pickle) are some of the specialities of this region. Being rather exotic in flavour, they are slowly entering the arena of Nepali cuisine and quite a few restaurants in Kathmandu are serving this far-eastern cuisine.

Yangben

Kaalo Bangur Ko Masu,
Bhatmas Ra Rayo

61

Kaalo Bangur Ko Masu, Bhatmas Ra Rayo

Pork, Soya Beans and Mustard Greens

Black pigs are bred in eastern Nepal, mainly Dharan, and are famous for their tasty meat. This preparation can be made with just the meat, omitting the mustard greens and soya beans.

Preparation time: 45 minutes
Serves: 8

INGREDIENTS

1 kg pork meat with skin and fat
3 tbsp. mustard oil
2 bay leaves
½ tsp. fenugreek seeds
1 cup sliced onions
2 cups chopped tomatoes
2 tbsp. onion paste
2 tbsp. coarsely crushed garlic
2 tbsp. coarsely crushed ginger
½ tsp. turmeric powder
3 tbsp. cumin powder
2 tbsp. coriander powder
1 ½ tbsp. red chilli powder
1 cup black beans soaked overnight in water/ fermented beans
1 big bunch fresh mustard greens
Salt to taste

PREPARATION

Soak the soya beans in water overnight or for a few hours to help them ferment. Slice the pork into 1 inch cubes, boil the soaked beans in a pressure cooker for 2 whistles until nearly done. Chop the mustard greens roughly, retaining the tender stems. Heat the oil in a heavy-bottomed pan till it smokes, add the fenugreek and bay leaves, wait till the seeds turn black then add the sliced onions. Fry till they turn a golden brown, then add the pork to the pan and keep stirring until the meat turns dark brown in colour and is half-cooked. Add the ground onions and ginger garlic paste to the meat and stir for 2 minutes. Finally, add the dry spices and cook again for a few minutes until the spices are well integrated with the meat. Add the tomatoes and beans to the meat and cover and cook until the oil separates from the pork. Add the roughly chopped mustard greens and stir till they wilt a little. Serve immediately so the greens remain crunchy.

Yangben

Wild Edible Lichen

Yangben, the edible lichen, originated in China's Yunnan region and travelled to eastern Nepal as early as the seventh century. It was easily foraged for in the jungles of the region and became an interesting accompaniment to pork meat and blood. Due to its high fibre content, it takes longer to digest, reducing the absorption of pork fat in the body. Khanakpa is a wild berry found in the region, which has a sharp taste but is milder than Sichuan pepper. These herbs and berries are now available in stores in Kathmandu. This dish is usually served as snacks or koseli (meaning gift), with tongba, the local drink, when entertaining guests.

Preparation time: 45 minutes
Serves: 8

INGREDIENTS

2 cups yangben
1 cup pork blood
2 khanakpa (wild herb/optional)
3 tbsp. mustard oil
½ tbsp. garlic paste
½ tbsp. ginger paste
½ tsp. cumin powder
½ tsp. red chilli powder
½ cup chopped green garlic shoots
Salt to taste

PREPARING THE YANGBEN

Clean the *yangben* and remove all dirt from it, soak it in cold water for an hour. Boil the *yangben* in 1 tsp. ash and 2 litres of water for 15 minutes till the lichen is soft, wash it a couple of times till it is clean of all the ash. The *yangben* can be cooked immediately after this process or sun-dried for later use.

PREPARATION

Mix all the ingredients and stir till no blood clots remain, heat mustard oil in a pan and add this mixture to the heated oil and keep stirring so it does not stick to the bottom of the pan. Once the water dries, it is ready for consumption.

Tarkari Haleko Yangben

Yangben with Vegetables

Preparation time: 20 minutes
Serves: 8

INGREDIENTS

2 cups mixed vegetables (cauliflower, potatoes,
carrots and beans)
1 cup yangben
3 tbsp. mustard oil
¼ tsp. fenugreek seeds
½ cup sliced onions
½ cup chopped tomatoes
½ tbsp. garlic paste
½ tbsp. ginger paste
½ tsp. turmeric powder
Salt to taste

PREPARATION

Prepare the *yangben* like in the recipe above, cut the vegetables in the same size. Heat the oil, temper the fenugreek seeds till black, then add the chopped vegetables and stir till well-coated with oil, cover and cook till half-cooked. Then add the onions, turmeric powder and salt and stir again for 2 minutes. Add the ginger garlic paste and tomatoes, cover and cook again till the vegetables are well cooked and the oil separates, add the *yangben* and mix well. Serve hot.

Kinema

Fermented Soya Beans

Preparation time: 45 minutes
Serves: 8

INGREDIENTS

½ kg dry soya beans
1 tbsp. mustard oil
2 green chillies
½ cup sliced onions
½ cup chopped tomatoes
½ tsp. turmeric powder
½ tsp. red chillies
Salt to taste
½ cup chopped green coriander and green
garlic shoots

FERMENTATION PROCESS OF KINEMA

Roast the soya beans in a thick-bottomed pan for
5 minutes on low heat, then pressure cook with 4 cups
hot water for 3 whistles. Prepare a *doko* (basket) made
out of cane, layered with banana, *saal* or pumpkin leaves.
Cool the beans and layer between the leaves and leave to
ferment for 3 days. Once they start smelling strong and
become sticky, lay the beans out and dry in the sun for
further use later. You can cook immediately as well.

PREPARATION

Heat the oil in a pan and add the green chillies, onions
and tomatoes, cook till the tomatoes are soft and mushy.
Add the salt, turmeric powder and 2 cups of the prepared
kinema, cook in 3 cups hot water in a pressure cooker for
4 whistles. Once the beans are well cooked and integrated
with the other ingredients, the *kinema* soup is ready to
serve.

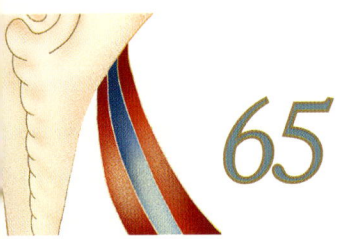

65

Chimping, Golbheda Ko Achar

Nepali Hogweed and Tomato Achar

Chimping is a dried seed used commonly in the preparing of food in the Rai Limbu communities, which serves medicinal purposes as well. It has a citrus, sharp, slightly bitter taste and is used for spicing curries and pickles.

Preparation time: 20 minutes
Serves: 6

INGREDIENTS

2 cups chopped tomatoes
1 tbsp. chimpimg
½ tsp. red chilli powder OR
1 dalle khursani (red cherry pepper chilli)
1 tbsp. mustard oil
Salt to taste

PREPARATION

Charcoal-roast the tomatoes and chop. Heat the oil and cook the tomatoes in it. Add all the ingredients to a mortar and pestle and grind roughly to incorporate all ingredients together. Serve as an accompaniment to rice and corn grits, meat and vegetables.

Philunge Ko Achar

Jhuse Til/Niger Seed Powder Pickle

This is a tasty pickle that can be eaten fresh or stored and served with a daal bhaat or dhindo meal.

Preparation time: 20 minutes
Serves: 4-6
Makes: 2 cups

INGREDIENTS

2 cups philunge (niger) seeds
4 dalle khursani (red cherry pepper chilli)
1 inch ginger
2 tbsp. lemon juice
Salt to taste

PREPARATION

Slowly smoke the chillies over a charcoal fire till they shrivel and turn black in colour. Coarsely grind the ginger, dry roast the *philunge* seeds and cool. Grind the *philunge* and chillies to a fine powder, mix all the ingredients and serve with a meal or store in a bottle.

THARU

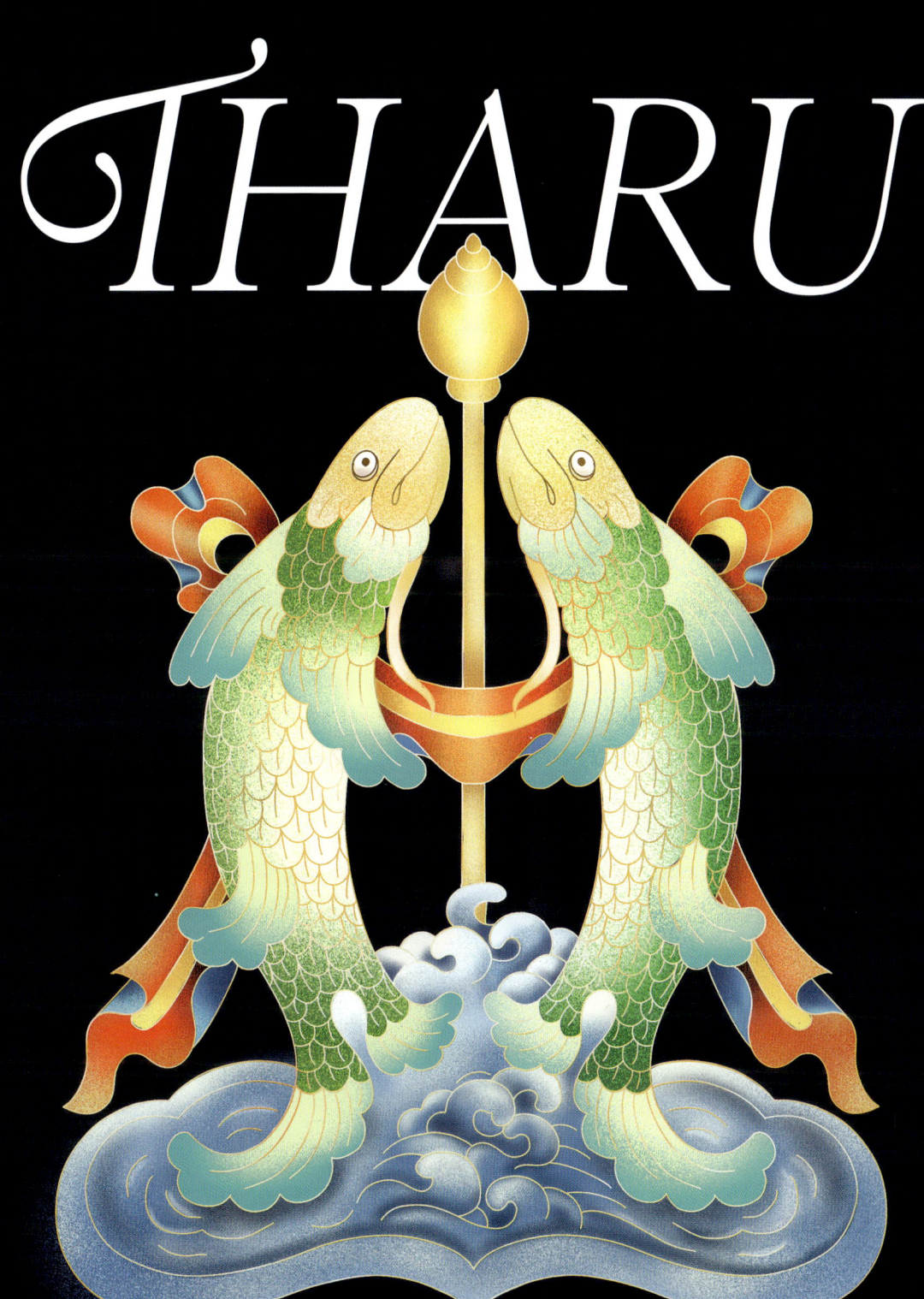

The Tharus is an indigenous ethnic community that has inhabited the western and southern region, spreading as far as the east of the Terai region of Nepal, for centuries. This community is believed to have come from the Thar desert of Rajasthan in India. Having lived and survived in the malarial jungles of the Terai, they remained isolated for a long time and thus have been able to retain their culture, religion and social practices from external influences. They mainly occupy six districts in Nepal: Dang, Banke, Bardia, Surkhet, Kailali and Kanchanpur. The Tharus are nature-worshippers, having a rich cultural heritage, and speak many dialects. They are agrarian in nature, cultivating rice, nearly always settling around the river banks to facilitate fishing and living off the produce in the jungles. The *Tharu* people use special fishing nets called *khauki jaal*, carried on the head, that are very differently styled in comparison to the common fishing nets.

Dhikari

Steamed Rice Flour Dough in Different Shapes

Preparation time: 45 minutes
Serves: 8

INGREDIENTS

1 kg anadi rice
3 cups water
1 tsp. small cardamom powder

PREPARATION

Mix the flour, water and cardamom powder into a smooth, soft dough. Take small pieces of dough in your hand and roll into an oblong shape; another shape is made by taking a piece of dough in the palm of your hand and rolling it with both hands, when it becomes round, flatten a little to make the shape in the picture. Special shapes like the thin *dhikari* in a bundle are made for religious offerings. Steam for 20 minutes, then check to see if the *dhikari* is cooked. This dish can be served hot or cold.

Tharu Aaloo

Bair Chutney

Anadi Chawal Ko Roti

Dhikari

Baria

Baria

Deef-Fried Lentil Cutlets

Preparation time: 1 hour
Serves: 10

INGREDIENTS

1 kg maas daal (black bean lentils)
2 cups maida (refined flour)
2 tbsp. garlic paste
2 tbsp. ginger paste
2 tsp. cumin powder
2 tsp. coriander powder
3 tsp. chilli powder
½ cup chopped coriander leaves
Salt to taste
Oil for deep-frying

PREPARATION

Soak the lentils overnight and rinse well. You can retain some skin as well for texture. Grind very coarsely, add the maida, ginger and garlic paste and spices, salt and chopped coriander, a little water and mix well. Place in a steamer, leave space in between the lentil mixture so the steam can pass through and cook the lentils. Steam for 30 minutes, the lentils should be cooked, cool for 5 minutes then take lumps of the mixture when still warm, press together and make thick oblong cylinders. It should stay together and not disintegrate when touched. Cut ½ inch discs with a sharp knife. Keep aside, heat oil in a wok and deep-fry till the *barias* are golden brown. Serve as snacks accompanied with *bair* chutney.

Anadi Chawal Ko Roti

Sweet Deep-Fried Rice Flour Bread

Preparation time: 20 minutes
Serves: 8

INGREDIENTS

1 kg anadi rice flour
1 cup sugar
Oil for deep-frying

PREPARATION

Add the sugar to the flour and keep kneading with ½ cup water, add more water and knead till you form a smooth dough. Make same-sized balls and roll out to make small discs and keep in a tray. Heat oil and slip in the discs and fry on both sides to a golden brown. Best eaten hot but can be stored for a week and served cold.

Surik Sekuwa

Sidra Macchi

Ghoongi

Ghoongi

Snail Curry

Preparation time: 45 minutes
Serves: 8

INGREDIENTS

1 kg snails
1 tsp. salt
½ cup rice flour
½ cup oil
¼ cup coarsely ground ginger
¼ cup coarsely ground garlic
½ tsp. turmeric powder
1 tsp. cumin powder
1 tsp. coriander powder
1 tsp. red chilli powder
2 tsp. coarsely ground timur
1 tbsp. rice flour
Salt to taste
½ cup chopped coriander leaves

PREPARATION

Mix ½ cup rice flour with snails and soak in water overnight. Next morning, rinse the snails well and boil in water with 1 tsp. salt and ½ tsp. turmeric powder for 15 minutes. Drain the water and snip the snail tips with a scissor, remove the small black pieces from the open ends. Heat oil in a heavy-bottomed pan and fry the ginger garlic paste and spices for 3 minutes, then add the snails, stir for 2 minutes add 2 cups water and cook for 30 minutes. Add 2 tbsp. rice flour in ½ cup water, blend and add to the pot of cooked snails. Once the gravy thickens, garnish with chopped coriander and serve.

Surik Sekuwa

Charcoal-Grilled Pork

Preparation time: 45 minutes
Serves: 6-8

INGREDIENTS

1 kg pork
2 tbsp. garlic paste
2 tbsp. ginger paste
2 tsp. coriander powder
1 ½ tsp. cumin powder
½ tsp. turmeric powder
1 ½ tsp. red chilli powder
1 tbsp. lemon juice
Salt to taste

PREPARATION

Slice the pork in 1 inch slices, mix all the ingredients with the meat and marinate for 1 hour. Charcoal-grill or deep-fry the meat according to taste. Any method tastes good.

Sidra Macchi

Deep-Fried and Tempered Small Fish

Preparation time: 30 minutes
Serves: 6

INGREDIENTS

3 cups small fish
½ cup chopped onions
1 tbsp. green chillies
1 tbsp. chopped tomatoes
¼ cup garlic
¼ cup ginger
½ tsp. red chilli powder
1 tsp. lemon juice
Salt to taste
Oil for deep-frying
¼ cup chopped coriander leaves

PREPARATION

Deep-fry the small fish and place in a bowl. Add all the ingredients and mix and serve, this dish can be served hot or cold.

Tharu Aaloo

Tharu Tempered Potatoes

Preparation time: 20 minutes
Serves: 6

INGREDIENTS

½ kg small potatoes
¼ cup oil
½ tsp. cumin seeds
Salt to taste
2 tbsp. chopped green garlic shoots

PREPARATION

Boil the potatoes and retain the skin. Heat oil and temper the cumin seeds till they pop. Then add the potatoes and salt, stir for 5 minutes and garnish with the garlic shoots.

Bair Chutney

Wild Indian Plum Chutney

Preparation time: 15 minutes
Serves: 6

INGREDIENTS

2 cups bair
4 tbsp. sugar
2 tsp. red chilli powder
Salt to taste
2 cups water

PREPARATION

Add all the ingredients to 2 cups of water and boil till the plums are cooked. This delicious chutney is the perfect accompaniment to a *Tharu* or any meal.

MADESH

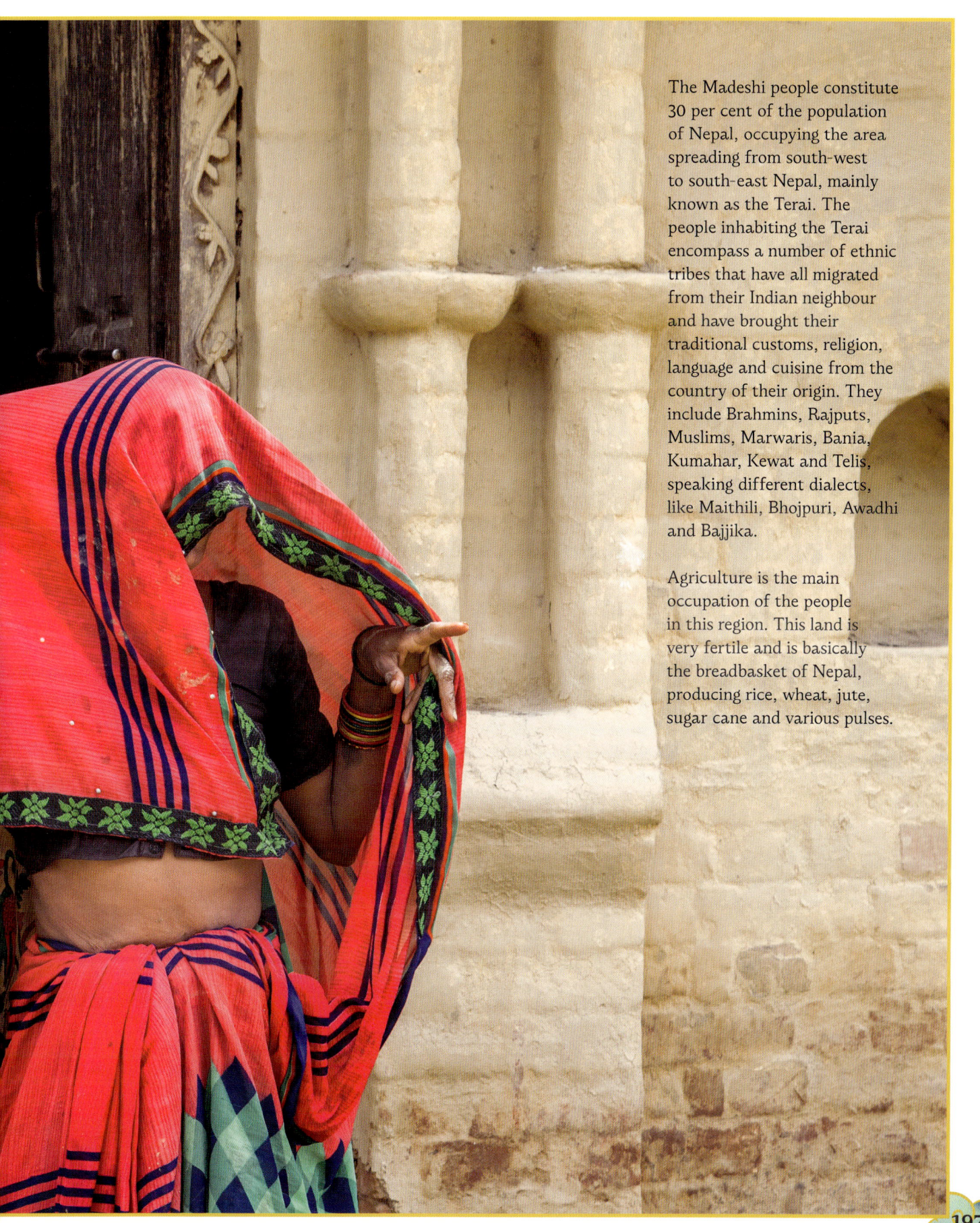

The Madeshi people constitute 30 per cent of the population of Nepal, occupying the area spreading from south-west to south-east Nepal, mainly known as the Terai. The people inhabiting the Terai encompass a number of ethnic tribes that have all migrated from their Indian neighbour and have brought their traditional customs, religion, language and cuisine from the country of their origin. They include Brahmins, Rajputs, Muslims, Marwaris, Bania, Kumahar, Kewat and Telis, speaking different dialects, like Maithili, Bhojpuri, Awadhi and Bajjika.

Agriculture is the main occupation of the people in this region. This land is very fertile and is basically the breadbasket of Nepal, producing rice, wheat, jute, sugar cane and various pulses.

75

Taas Ko Masu

Spicy Dry Mutton

Preparation time: 45 minutes
Serves: 8

INGREDIENTS

1 kg mutton cubes
1 cup mustard oil
¼ cup coriander seeds
¼ cup cumin seeds
10 red chillis
1 tsp. timur powder
1 tsp. turmeric powder
1 tsp. garam masala
½ cup coarsely crushed garlic
½ cup coarsely crushed ginger
3 tbsps. lemon juice
¼ cup julienned garlic
¼ cup julienned ginger
Salt to taste

GARNISHING

½ cup finely chopped green onions
¼ cup chopped coriander leaves

PREPARATION

Chop the mutton into 1 inch cubes and keep aside. In a heavy-bottomed pan, add coriander, cumin and red chillies, dry roast on medium heat till the spices are fragrant and a light golden colour. Cool and roughly grind in a mortar and pestle or grinder. Mix all the ingredients with the mutton. Marinate overnight and mix again and keep aside. Heat the oil till it smokes and add the marinated meat mixture to the pan. Cook on low heat and keep stirring till the oil separates and the meat is a dark brown colour. When the meat is cooked, remove the pieces of meat from the pan, leaving the oil and spices in the pan. Take out the spice mixture and keep aside. In a small pan, add oil and fry the julienned garlic and ginger to a golden brown; add to the meat. Serve the meat with an accompaniment of *bhuja* (puffed rice) topped with the cooked spice mixture, garnished with green onions and coriander leaves.

Mula Ko Achar

Radish Pickle

This tasty achar is an accompaniment to the Taas Ko Masu. It graces a typical Nepali thaali meal as well.

Preparation time: 30 minutes
Serves: 6

INGREDIENTS

2 cups radish
3 green chillies
1 tbsp. chopped garlic
1 ½ cups chopped tomatoes
½ tsp. cumin seeds
1 tsp. red chilli powder
½ tsp. turmeric powder
½ tsp. timur
3 tbsp. mustard oil
Salt to taste
1 tbsp. chopped coriander leaves for garnish

PREPARATION

Cut radish into 2 inch sticks, slit the chillies lengthways in half, chop the tomatoes into small cubes. Heat oil and splutter the cumin seeds, add chopped garlic and green chillies. Add turmeric, red chilli powder, *timur* and tomatoes and cook till tomatoes are mushy, now add the radish and cook for 5 minutes till radish is cooked but still crunchy. Serve hot or cold, garnished with chopped coriander leaves.

Katiya Masu

Mutton Cooked in an Earthen Pot

This popular dish originates from the Rautahat area of the Terai. A wooden stick is used to stir the meat in the pot because the pot is stuffed with the meat and spices to the brim, a spoon would have no manoeuvring space.

Preparation time: 2 hours
Serves: 2 persons per pot

INGREDIENTS

250 grams mutton
3 tbsp. mustard oil
1 large sliced onion
2 whole red chillies
1 whole garlic
2 bay leaves
1 tsp. whole garam masala
½ tsp. garam masala powder
½ tsp. whole coriander seeds
½ tsp. cumin seeds
1 tsp. turmeric powder
½ tsp. fennel seeds
Salt to taste
1 tsp. ghee for garnishing

PREPARATION

Prepare a medium earthen clay pot and glaze with some oil. Place all the ingredients except the *ghee* in a bowl and mix well, spoon into the pot and fill it to the brim. Push the meat in with a thin wooden spoon or stick, keep pushing and slowly mixing so that the meat, spices and onions are well integrated. Close the lid and seal with dough so no steam escapes, cook slowly on a medium coal fire for 2 hours. Every 30 minutes open and mix the meat around with the stick. After 1 hour, place a whole garlic pod on top. After 2 hours, check to see if the meat is cooked and oil is separated and floating on top. Charcoal-grill the garlic pod and use as a garnish or squeeze out the garlic cloves and mix with the meat. When the meat is ready, add 1 tsp. *ghee* to the pot, mix well and serve.

Tarkari Ko Achar

Chawal Ko Roti

Chawal Ko Roti

Rice Flour Bread

Preparation time: 45 minutes
Serves: 8-10

INGREDIENTS

3 cups rice flour
3 cups water

FILLING
1 cup chana daal (Bengal gram)
½ tsp. turmeric powder
1 tbsp. mustard oil
2-3 whole red chillies
1 tsp. cumin seeds
1 tbsp. coarsely ground garlic
Salt to taste
2 tsp. oil for sautéeing
Mustard/vegetable oil for deep-frying

PREPARATION

Heat 3 cups water in a saucepan till it boils. Add the rice flour and mix well, cover the pan and keep aside for 10 minutes. Boil the *chana daal* in 2 cups of water with the turmeric powder for 5 minutes. Strain the water and keep aside. Heat the oil in a pan and add the cumin seeds and whole chillies to the pan and sauté. Add the *daal,* salt and garlic to the pan and mix well, cook for 2 minutes and take off the fire. Cool and grind to a fine powder. Knead the rice flour with the heel of your palm and make into a smooth dough. Divide into equal portions and make into a disc with a dent in the middle, add 2 tsp. of the lentil filling and slowly close the dough over the stuffing. Place a plastic sheet over the disc then with the palm of your hand press and move it anti-clockwise to flatten out the disc to make a 4 inch diameter. This method prevents the filling from spilling out of the rice flour covering. Smooth the edges with your fingertips. Keep the discs in a tray, heat the oil and fry one at a time till it puffs and cooks on one side, flip it to the other side to cook in the same way. These delicious *rotis* taste best when eaten hot.

Tarkari Ko Achar

Mixed Vegetable Pickle

Preparation time: 45 minutes
Serves: 8

INGREDIENTS

2 cups cubed potatoes
2 cups cubed carrots
2 cups cauliflower florets
2 cups beans
4 tbsp. mustard oil
2 tbsp. panch phoran seeds (mixture of fennel, carom, cumin, fenugreek and nigella seeds)
1 tsp. mustard seeds
1 tsp. yellow mustard seeds
1 tbsp. red chilli powder
1 tsp. turmeric powder
Juice of 2 lemons
Salt to taste

PREPARATION

Cut the carrots, cauliflower and beans into same-sized cubes and steam till cooked but firm, dry thoroughly. Boil and cut the potatoes in same size as the other vegetables. Dry roast all the spices in a pan, except the red chillies and turmeric, cool and grind the spices roughly. Place all the ingredients except oil in a pan and mix well. Heat 3 tbsp. mustard oil in a small pan till it smokes, take it off the fire and add the turmeric powder, swirl to mix, and add the oil to the pan with the vegetables. Add 1 tbsp. raw mustard oil and mix further. Serve immediately or store in the refrigerator in an airtight jar for a week.

This recipe can be made with just potatoes and beans.

Aaloo Chokha

Spiced Potatoes

Preparation time: 15 minutes
Serves: 4

INGREDIENTS

4 medium potatoes
3 tbsp. chopped onions
1 tsp. chopped green chillies
2 tsp. chopped green coriander
1 tsp. crushed red chillies
1 ½ tbsp. mustard oil
Salt to taste

PREPARATION

Boil and mash the potatoes, add all the ingredients in a bowl and mix well. Serve as it is or make balls for better presentation.

Litti

Wheat Balls Stuffed with Spiced Lentils

Littis were originally cooked over coal fire or goitha, disc-like briquettes made out of cow dung and hay. They were placed between burning briquettes and baked till cooked, then placed in a jute sack and shaken till the ash was rubbed off them.

Preparation time: 45 minutes
Serves: 4
2 littis per person

INGREDIENTS

2 cups wheat flour
1 tbsp. oil
1 ½ tsp. salt

FILLING

10 tbsp. sattu (roasted gram flour)
1 tbsp. chopped onions
1 ½ tbsp. chopped garlic
1 ½ tbsp. chopped ginger
2 tbsp. chopped green coriander
1 ½ tsp. chopped green chillies
1 tsp. carom seeds
2 tbsp. lime juice
2 tbsp. mustard oil
Salt to taste

PREPARATION

Place the flour, salt and *ghee* in a basin and rub with fingertips to resemble breadcrumbs. Slowly add water and knead into a soft, pliable dough. Keep aside for 30 minutes. Add all the ingredients of the filling in a bowl and mix well. Make 8 even balls of dough and place in a plate. Make a small disc with a hollow in the middle and add 2 tbsp. of the mixture in it, slowly close the edges over the filling tightly and shape into a ball. Heat oven, place the *littis* in a greased tray and bake for 5-10 minutes till they are cooked. You could bake them in a coal fire, if feeling adventurous.

Break the *littis* in half and serve with hot *ghee* over them. Mutton curry or eggplant/potato *chokha* is the perfect accompaniment to these delicious balls.

Aaloo Chokha

Litti

Thekuwa

Sweet Biscuits

Preparation time: 40 minutes
Serves: 10

INGREDIENTS

2 cups wheat flour
1 cup maida (refined flour)
⅓ cup ghee
1 cup sugar
1 tbsp. fennel seeds
2 tbsp. grated coconut (optional)
Oil for frying

PREPARATION

Place both types of flour in a bowl. Add *ghee* and mix with your fingertips till the mixture resembles breadcrumbs. Add the sugar, fennel seeds and grated coconut and mix. Take half a fistful of the flour, sprinkle a little water on it and try and bind it by pressing hard together in the palm of one hand with the fingers. Take two balls in both hands and press together till they bind together in an oblong shape and not crumble. Oil the mould and press the oblong balls of flour on it to take its imprint and shape, smoothen the sides so they have no cracks. If a mould is not available, place the pressed flour cake on the table and make imprints with a fork. Fry each *thekuwa* on medium heat to a reddish-brown colour. Tastes best served hot but can be kept in an airtight container for a few weeks.

Maal Puwa

Crispy Fried Pancakes

Preparation time: 30 minutes
Serves: 10, Makes: 20

INGREDIENTS

4 cups refined flour
⅓ cup ghee
2 cups sugar
3 ½ cups milk
2 tbsp. fennel seeds
1 cup mashed bananas (optional)

PREPARATION

Sieve the flour, add the *ghee* and rub together with your fingertips till it resembles breadcrumbs. Add the milk and blend with a hand mixer till there are no lumps and you have a smooth batter. Add the sugar and blend again till it is well integrated, add the fennel seeds and mashed bananas. Refrigerate the batter overnight or for 5 hours minimum. Heat oil to medium heat in a flat-bottomed pan and gently add a ladle of the beaten batter to the pan, you can fry 3-4 at a time. Flip to the other side once they are fried to nice golden brown. Serve hot or with an accompaniment of clotted cream and garnish with dry fruits.

MITHILA

The wedding of Ram and Sita in Mithila style

The name Mithila refers to the ancient Videha kingdom of the eleventh century. The town Janakpur is famous as the birthplace of Goddess Sita from the epic Ramayana. The Mithila form of art is extremely popular, practised mainly by the local women of the area, with its history dating as far back as the twelfth century. This beautiful art form is said to have originated when King Janak ordered his subjects to paint the town to celebrate his daughter Sita's wedding to Lord Ram of Ayodhya. This form of art celebrates women empowerment through the ages.

The regional language is known as Maithili and the festivals of Maghe, Holi and Chhat are celebrated with great fervour.

The food is typical of its southern neighbour but includes the *daal bhaat* cuisine of Nepal with an addition of fish and vegetables prepared in its unique Maithili flavour.

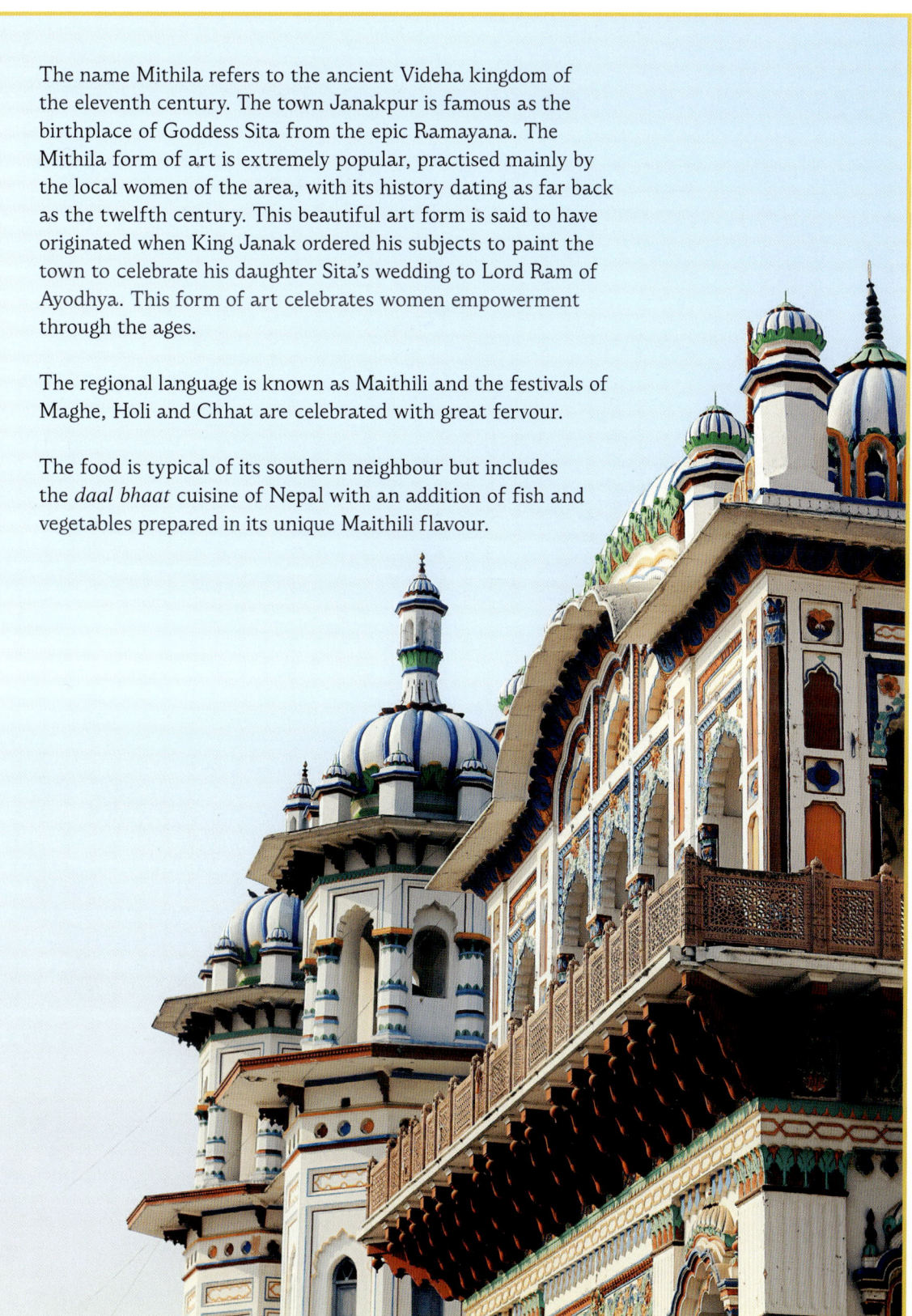

Machha Ke Jhor

Fish Curry

Fish is cooked all over the Terai area, but this dish hails from Janakpur. The use of Kashmiri mirch, kasuri methi and panch phoran is evidence of the influence on the cuisine by its southern neighbour.

Preparation time: 45 minutes
Serves: 6

INGREDIENTS

1 kg rohu fish cut in 2 inch pieces
1 ½ cup mustard oil
1 tsp. fenugreek seeds
2 bay leaves
½ cup yellow mustard seeds (sarson)
1 tsp. turmeric powder
2 tsp. coriander powder
2 tsp. Kashmiri mirch powder
1 ¼ cups onion paste
2 large tomatoes
5 cloves garlic
1 inch ginger
1 tsp. kasuri methi
Salt to taste
1 tsp. panch phoran

PREPARATION

Soak the mustard seeds in a cup of water for 1 hour and grind to a paste. Cut the fish into eleven 2 inch round pieces and marinate in salt and turmeric powder for 1 hour. Heat oil in a heavy-bottomed pan and fry the fish to a deep golden brown colour. Remove the fish and keep aside. Leave ¼ cup oil in the pan, add the bay leaves and fenugreek seeds and wait for the seeds to turn dark brown before adding the ground onion and garlic paste. Fry for 2-3 minutes till the raw smell dissipates. Add the mustard paste and keep stirring for 5 minutes. In 1 cup of water, add the coriander, red chilli and turmeric powders and mix well, then add to the pan and stir for another few minutes. Cook for 5 minutes then add ½ cup oil and the tomatoes, keep cooking till the oil separates and the mixture is a nice red colour. This can take 15 minutes. Add salt according to taste. Once it starts sticking to the pan, add hot water and mix to a nice fluid consistency, let it come to a boil and gently add the fried fish to the gravy. Reduce heat and let it cook till the oil floats on top and the gravy thickens. Add *kasuri methi* and chopped coriander leaves as garnish.

OPTIONAL

Heat 1 tbsp. of oil and add 1 tsp. of *panch phoran* to it, take off the fire and add 1 tsp. of red Kashmiri chilli powder, swirl in the oil and pour over the fish curry just before serving.

Taral Maach

Fried Fish

Preparation time: 30 minutes
Serves: 6

INGREDIENTS

1 kg rohu fish
1 tbsp. ginger paste
1 tbsp. garlic paste
1 tsp. turmeric powder
2 tsp. coriander powder
2 tsp. cumin powder
2 tsp. red chilli powder
3 tbsp. lemon juice
¼ cup yogurt
1 tbsp. besan (chickpea flour)
2 tbsp. rice flour
Salt to taste
Mustard/vegetable oil for frying

PREPARATION

Cut the fish in 2 ½ inch round pieces. Place all the spices in a bowl and mix well with the fish and marinate for 2 hours. Heat oil and deep-fry on medium heat till the fish is a golden brown colour. Remove from the pan and serve hot with wedges of lime and fried green chillies.

Taruwa

Deep-Fried Vegetables Coated in Rice Flour

Preparation time: 30 minutes
Serves: 6

INGREDIENTS

6 cauliflower florets
2 large potatoes
1 large brinjal
1 yam
¼ pumpkin
1 bunch of tilkor leaves (pointed gourd leaves)
3 cups rice soaked overnight
¼ cup wheat|gram flour
½ tsp. garam masala
1 tsp. cumin powder
1 tsp. turmeric powder
½ tsp. red chilli powder
1 tsp. garlic paste
Salt to taste
Oil for frying

PREPARATION

Soak rice overnight in a cup of water. Grind to a smooth paste with a little water, mix the rice flour, garlic paste and spices and whisk to form a thick batter. Slice the vegetable to ¼ inch slices, make a small slit in the stems of the cauliflowers and keep aside. Heat the oil, then dip the vegetables in the batter and coat evenly on all sides then fry to a golden brown on medium heat. Fry the cauliflowers stem facing down to ensure they cook from inside. Tastes best served hot.

Bhanti

Kadima

Kadima

Sautéed Pumpkin and Peas

Preparation time: 20 minutes
Serves: 6

INGREDIENTS

5 cups pumpkin
½ cup peas
2 tbsp. oil
2 red chillies
½ tsp. fenugreek seeds
½ tsp. turmeric powder
Salt to taste

PREPARATION

Slice the pumpkin into 1 inch pieces. Heat the oil and add the fenugreek seeds, cook till they turn a dark brown then add the chillies and pumpkin to the pan and stir. Add all the other ingredients and mix well, cover and cook till the pumpkin is soft but not mushy, add the peas and cook for 2 minutes, garnish with chopped green coriander and serve hot.

Bhanti

Sautéed Eggplants

Preparation time: 30 minutes
Serves: 6

INGREDIENTS

4 big round eggplants
2 chopped green chillies
Juice of 1 lemon
4 tbsp. chopped onions
1 tbsp. coarsely ground ginger
1 tbsp. coarsely ground garlic
½ tsp. turmeric powder
1 tbsp. panch phoran
2 tbsp. mustard oil
Salt to taste

PREPARATION

Charcoal-grill the eggplants, preferably; if coal not available, on a gas top till the skin is seared black. Remove the charred skin and chop the flesh into small pieces. Place the chopped green chillies, onions, salt and lemon juice in a bowl with the eggplant and mix well. Heat oil in a tempering pan and add the *panch phoran* and crushed garlic ginger to the oil and cook till it is a golden colour, remove from heat and add the turmeric powder, swirl in the oil and pour over the eggplants and mix well. This dish is served at room temperature.

MOMOS

Momo! The name itself conjures bliss and gratification. The second these tiny morsels of deliciousness hit the taste buds and the juice oozes into the mouth, one is transported into a virtual explosion of flavours, resulting in an instant 'foodgasm'.

Whatever name one gives these delectable dumplings, in China they are known as *jiaozi, gyoza* in Japan, *mandu* in Korea, *manti* in Türkiye, *ravioli* in Italy and originally *momocha* in Nepal, they have become the most popular dish around the world.

The two versions of the origin of *momos,* both start and end in Nepal.

One story of the *momo's* origin begins early in the fourteenth century, when Nepalese princess Bhrikuti married the Tibetan King Tsong Tsang Gampo. She took with her Nepalese art, architecture, religion and culture to propagate in her new Tibetan home. The tiny *momo* travelled with her as part of her culinary dowry.

The other story travels with the Newari tradesmen on their trade route to and fro, from Lhasa in Tibet to Kathmandu. While conducting their business there they ate a dish of delicious dumplings called *mog mog*. These steamed flour dumplings were stuffed with yak meat. They brought back this easily prepared dish and adapted it to their taste and palate using buffalo meat and serving it with a spicy tomato sesame sauce. It was renamed from *mug mug* to the Newari *ma neu* meaning 'easily steamed', to *momocha* and finally to the name it is most commonly known by: *momo*.

The versatile *momo* comes in different sizes, shapes and fillings, easily adaptable to one's culinary preferences. You can steam, boil, sauté or deep-fry them, or in the tune of fusion cooking, you can pan fry, barbecue or bake them.

Basically, the *momo* is a dumpling made out of thinly rolled flour dough, stuffed with the filling of your choice and steamed for a few minutes, served steaming hot accompanied with a spicy sauce. The region in which these dumplings are prepared ascertains the filling and the flour used. The Himalayan region uses yak meat and a thick wheat or buckwheat flour covering. The Kathmandu valley, where it was originally consumed, used buffalo meat and refined flour for the wrapper. Mutton, pork and chicken fillings are popular and now even fish and prawn are slowly taking over as healthier options. As vegetarianism is growing and healthy eating is gaining in popularity, vegetable stuffings of spinach, cabbage, zucchini, carrots and mushrooms lie happily nestled in the *momo* stuffing. Cottage and other cheeses are also being added to the *momo* repertoire and tickle the taste buds further, with accompanying soups and fresh pickles. These tasty *achars* are typically made out of tomatoes spiced with red chillies, *til* (sesame) and *timur* (Sichuan pepper). There are a variety of accompaniments that have hit the momo-manic market and add deliciously to the gourmandizing that accompanies consuming *momos*. The outer layer of dough is rolled as thinly as possible, enabling one to taste more of the rich filling rather than the covering.

I have experimented with a few fusion recipes incorporating *momos* to make it as versatile as possible to suit various palates and tastes. One can never have enough of this delectable dumpling! MOMOS, MOMOS AND MORE MOMOS...

Momo Wrapper

Momo wrappers are as important to the taste of the dumpling as the filling. The thinner the dough wrapper, the more the taste of the filling is intensified and the momo melts in the mouth. If rolled too thin, they break in the process of steaming and the juices ooze out into the pan rather than in the mouth—a total disaster! The plain flour wrappers are the most popular, but healthier options are taking its place, such as whole wheat and buckwheat flour, plain flour kneaded with the juice of colourful vegetables instead of plain water, giving it a more vibrant, healthier twist as well as allowing one to relish this sinful delicacy without guilt. The final option is making wrappers using cabbage and spinach leaves for the health addicts.

Preparation time: 30 minutes
Serves: 8-10, Makes: 60 Momos

INGREDIENTS

1 ½ cups maida (refined flour)
½ cup water
Pinch of salt

PREPARATION

Place the flour in a basin and slowly add the water to it, kneading it into a smooth dough. Be careful not let it get too soft, it should be of a firm consistency. Form the kneaded dough into a ball and dab a little oil on its surface, cover with a damp muslin cloth and let it rest for 2 hours. Remove the cloth and knead again, take a fistful of dough in your palm and roll out into a round, long disc of 1 inch thickness, cut ½ inch discs and form into small round balls, roll out each into a small disc as thin as possible, taking care that it does not tear while filling with stuffing.

VARIATION

Blend the vegetable of your choice with some water to help liquidize and blend to a thin, pouring consistency. Use the juice of the vegetable of your choice, like spinach, beetroot and carrots, to knead the dough to make beautiful colourful *momos*.

237

Various Ways to Make Momos

STEAMING

The original and most popular method of preparing *momos* is steaming. This is the easiest way to make momos as well and enables the optimum taste of the filling and juices of the *momos.*

KOTHE/PAN-FRIED

In this method, the previously steamed *momos* are pan-fried. Heat a pan and glaze with oil, place the flat part of the *momos* on the pan and let them cook for 2 minutes, until they get crispy and golden brown underneath.

SIU MAI

Siu mai is an open *momo* and is beautifully crafted with four openings to accommodate four different types of achars. Made in the same way as the other round *momos,* the edges of the wrapper are pinched together keeping open four small compartments.

DEEP-FRIED CRISPY MOMOS

Variations of the traditional steamed *momos* are becoming popular nowadays, adding new ways to eat the same delicious dumplings in tweaked ways. In this method, everything is the same as in the original recipe, except that the *momo* is deep-fried in hot oil instead of being steamed, giving a nice crisp, crunchy texture to the momos. One can fry them plain or roll them in breadcrumbs, vermicelli or panko to give an extra crunch.

1

Make small, equal, round balls and keep aside.

2

Roll out each dough ball into a small disc, as thin as possible.

3

Take the disc in your hand and put 1 tsp. filling in it.

4

Fold one side over and press both the edges together.

ng Momos

5

Press the edges together and pinch and overlap to make a design.

6

Rest the filled *momos* for a few minutes.

7

Oil the base of the steamer and place the *momos* in it.

8

Steam for 15 minutes.

Vegetable Momo

Preparation time: 30 minutes
Serves: 4, Makes: 20

PREPARATION

Mix all the ingredients and keep aside for 15–30 minutes. Roll out small discs and fill with 1 tsp. of the mixture, make the shape of your choice and steam for 15 minutes. Serve with the *achar* of your choice.

INGREDIENTS 1

1 cup mozzarella cheese
1 cup cream cheese
1 tsp. pepper powder
1 tbsp. chopped green onions
Salt to taste

INGREDIENTS 2

½ cup paneer (cottage cheese)/tofu
¼ cup grated cheese
1 cup finely chopped spinach
1 tsp. garlic paste
1 tsp. ginger paste
1 tbsp. spring onions
1 tsp. coriander powder
1 tsp. cumin powder
½ tsp. momo masala (if available)
Salt to taste

INGREDIENTS 3

½ cup finely chopped mushrooms
½ cup finely chopped cabbage
½ cup chopped cauliflower
½ cup finely chopped zucchini
½ cup grated carrots
1 tbsp. chopped onions
1 tbsp. chopped green coriander
1 tbsp. chopped green onions
1 tsp. garlic paste
1 tsp. ginger paste
1 tsp. cumin powder
1 tsp. coriander powder
1 tbsp. oil
Salt to taste

Momocha

Newari Momo

The ancient momo recipe that originated from the Newari community is called momocha, meaning small. The original round-shaped dumplings accompanied with golbheda achar are the most popular to date.

Preparation time: 1 hour
Serves: 8-10
Makes: 50 small momochas

INGREDIENTS

½ kg minced buffalo with fat
50 grams bone marrow
¼ cup chopped onion/shallots
1 tsp. garlic paste
1 tsp. ginger paste
1 tsp. cumin powder
2 tsp. roasted mustard oil
1 tsp. red chilli powder
1 tbsp. water
Salt to taste

PREPARATION

Mix all the ingredients and refrigerate for 1-2 hours. Take out, fill 1 tsp. of the mixture in the dumpling wrappers and make a round shape. Steam for 15 minutes.

Chicken Momo

Preparation time: 45 minutes
Serves: 8-10
Makes: 50 small momos

INGREDIENTS

½ kg minced chicken
2 tbsp. finely chopped shallots
2 tbsp. finely chopped onions
2 tbsp. chopped green coriander
2 tsp. garlic paste
2 tsp. ginger paste
1 tsp. coriander powder
1 tsp. cumin powder
2 tsp. momo masala (if available)
3 tbsp. oil
¼ cup frozen chicken stock/water
Salt to taste

PREPARATION

Mix all the ingredients well and keep aside to marinate for 30 minutes or longer, so all the spices integrate well. If you have used the chicken stock, keep the mixture in the refrigerator. Roll out the dough into small discs as thin as possible, fill 1 tsp. of the mixture into the discs, make the shape of your choice and steam for 15 minutes. Serve hot with your favourite *achar,* and consume immediately for optimum taste.

Mutton/Pork Momo

Preparation time: 45 minutes
Serves: 8-10
Makes: 50 small momos

INGREDIENTS

½ kg minced mutton/pork with fat
2 tbsp. chopped onions
2 tsp. chopped shallots
2 tbsp. chopped green onions
2 tbsp. chopped coriander leaves
2 ½ tsp. cumin powder
2 tsp. momo masala
2 tsp. garlic paste
2 tsp. ginger paste
4 tbsp. oil
Salt to taste

PREPARATION

Mix all the ingredients well and keep covered for 1 hour. Roll out thin discs, stuff mixture in the dough discs and make the shape of your choice. Steam for 20 minutes and serve hot with your favourite *achar*. Making *kothe* for this recipe is also recommended.

Mutton

Chicken

Pork

Fish

Buff

Jhol Momo

Momos Served in a Soup

Any momo of your choice can be served with the following soups.

Preparation time: 30 minutes
Serves: 4

INGREDIENTS

4 tbsp. sesame seeds
2 tbsp. bhatmas (dried soya beans)
2 tbsp. oil
½ tsp. cumin seeds
¼ tsp. carom seeds
4 tsp. chopped garlic
2 tsp. chopped onions
6-7 chopped tomatoes
3 chopped green chillies
½ tsp. coriander powder
½ tsp. cumin powder
¼ tsp. turmeric powder
1 tbsp. garlic ginger paste
Salt to taste

PREPARATION

Roast the sesame and soya bean seeds, cool and grind to a fine powder. Heat the oil and add the cumin and carom seeds and let them turn brown add the chopped garlic, onions and green chillies and sauté till the onions are translucent. Add the dry spices and cook for 2 minutes till raw smell dissipates, add the chopped tomatoes and salt and cook covered on medium heat for 5 minutes till tomatoes are cooked and mushy. Cool and grind to a fine paste, pour back into the pan and add the ground sesame and soya bean powder and 1-2 cups of water. Cook till it boils and is the right consistency. This soup can be thick or thin according to your personal taste. Add more water to make it thinner, adjust the salt.

Til Ko Jhol
(Sesame Seed Soup)
Omit the tomatoes from the ingredients and cook exactly like the above recipe.

Chara/Khasi/Buff Ko Ras

Chicken/Mutton/Buff Soup

Preparation time: 30 minutes
Serves: 4

INGREDIENTS

250 grams of chicken/mutton/buff meat with bones
1 chopped onion
2 tbsp. garlic cloves
2 tbsp. roughly chopped ginger
1 tomato
2 bay leaves
3 small cardamoms
1 small stick cinnamon
¼ tsp. turmeric powder
½ tsp. cumin powder
¼ tsp. red chilli powder
Salt to taste

PREPARATION

Cut the meat and bones in big pieces and place all the ingredients in a heavy-bottomed pan or pressure cooker. Add 4 cups water and cook on low heat for 30 minutes. Once the soup is cooked and the meat falls away from the bones, shred the meat and strain the soup in another pan. Add water if necessary, boil the prepared *momos* in this soup till they float on top or steam separately and add to the soup. Serve steaming hot, garnished with finely chopped shredded meat, spring onions and chilli oil.

Kwati Ko Jhol Momo

Momos in Sprouted Bean Soup

This sprouted bean momo soup is a tasty, nutritious 'all-in-one' healthy meal.
Great comfort food on a cold winter evening!

Preparation time: 45 minutes
Serves: 4-6

INGREDIENTS

12 steamed momos
2 cups sprouted beans
¼ cup mustard oil
¼ tsp. fenugreek seeds
¼ tsp. carom seeds
2 bay leaves
1 cup sliced onions
4 cups meat/vegetable stock
1 tbsp. garlic paste
1 tbsp. ginger paste
½ cup chopped tomatoes
1 tsp. coriander powder
1 tsp. cumin powder
½ tsp. turmeric powder
1 tsp. red chilli powder
Salt to taste

GARNISHING

¼ cup chopped coriander leaves
2 lemons cut in wedges

PREPARATION

Soak the sprouted beans in water overnight. Heat the mustard oil in a heavy-bottomed pan till it smokes, add the bay leaves, carom and fenugreek seeds. When the seeds splutter, add the sliced onions and sauté till a golden brown, then add the ground garlic and ginger paste and cook for 1 minute, add the dry spices and tomatoes and stir till the oil separates. Add the sprouted beans and cook till well coated with the spices, add 4 cups of stock or water and pressure cook the bean soup for 3-4 whistles till the beans are cooked and soft. Add the steamed *momos* of your choice and garnish with the coriander leaves with the lemon wedges on the side. An option is to cook the raw *momos* in the soup: add the *momos* to the soup and cook till they float on top.

Tingmo

Steamed Bun

*This delicious bun is eaten plain with an accompanying sauce or with hot,
steaming soups. Dhapu momo and shogo shabril momo are variations of the
same Tingmo using the same flour base with different fillings.*

Preparation time: 60 minutes
Serves: 5-6
Makes 6 Tingmos

INGREDIENTS

2 cups maida (refined flour)
1 tbsp. yeast
1 tsp. baking powder
1 tsp. salt
1 cup lukewarm water
1 tsp. oil

PREPARATION

Place the yeast in a bowl with the lukewarm water and let
the bubbles appear on top. Add all the ingredients, mix and
knead well with the heel of your palms, folding over again
and again to activate the gluten. Spread a little oil on the
surface and place in a covered bowl, proof in a warm place
for 1 hour. It should rise to double its original size, punch
it down and roll into a rectangular shape, oil the entire
surface well, fold its longer side into three, oiling each side
before overlapping. Use a knife to cut into four equal parts,
cut ½ inch thin strips of each part. Stack three strips over
three strips. Hold the edges together and gently pull and
stretch the strips, flipping them slowly and twisting them
to form a swirl, gently roll and tuck the edge under the
bun. Keep aside to proof again for 30 minutes, place in a
well-oiled steaming dish and steam for 15 minutes. Eat like
bread or accompanied by an *achar* or soup.

Shogo Shabril Momo

Tibetan Potato Meat Momos

This is a version of shogo shabril, which is a Tibetan croquette made with boiled potatoes and cooked minced meat. The original dish is adapted and the ingredients filled inside a momo and steamed.

Preparation time: 45 minutes
Serves: 6

INGREDIENTS

WRAPPER
Recipe No. 96 (Tingmo)

FILLING
½ kg minced meat if your choice
1 cup boiled, chopped potatoes
2 tbsp. chopped onions
1 tbsp. chopped garlic
1 tsp. chopped ginger
1 tbsp. soya sauce
¼ cup oil
1 tsp. coarsely ground pepper
Salt to taste

PREPARATION

Heat the oil in a pan and sauté the chopped garlic and onions till translucent, add the garlic, ginger paste and cook for a few minutes till raw smell dissipates. Add the minced meat, salt, pepper and soya sauce, and cook till the meat is done and changes colour, keep aside. Boil and chop the potatoes in cubes, add salt to taste and mix with the mince meat. Roll out the dough balls and add 2 tbsp. of the mixture in the middle of the disc. Pinch the edges together and steam for 20 minutes, serve hot!

Dhapu Momo

Giant Momo

Preparation time: 45 minutes
Serves: 4-6, Makes: 6

INGREDIENTS

WRAPPER
Recipe No. 96 (Tingmo)

FILLING
Recipe No. 97 (Shogo Shabril)
Omitting the potatoes
3 boiled eggs

PREPARATION

Make the dough exactly like *tingmo,* take 2 tbsps. dough to make large *momos* and roll to ¼ inch thickness in the shape of a disc. Take 2 tbsp. cooked minced meat (like for *shogo shabril momo)* filling of your choice and put in the middle of the disc, place half a boiled egg in the centre. Pinch the edges over to cover the filling and make a round shape. Keep aside for 30 minutes to proof, letting the dough rise. Steam for 20 minutes and serve with the *achar* of your choice or *timur chope.*

Rose Momo

Preparation time: 45 minutes
Serves: 6

INGREDIENTS

2 cups maida (refined flour)
1 cup beetroot/carrot/spinach juice
Filling of your choice (vegetable/chicken)

PREPARATION

ONE-COLOUR MOMO

The entire rose *momo* can be of one colour—use the vegetable juice of your choice (carrot, beetroot or spinach) to knead the dough, cover with a muslin cloth and keep aside for 30 minutes. Make a thin, long cylinder 1 inch in diameter, cut ½ inch pieces and roll out into thin discs.

TWO-COLOURED MOMOS

If you are making a two-coloured rose, divide the flour into two bowls. In bowl 1, pour the water and knead the dough according to original wrapper recipe on page 236. In bowl 2, slowly pour the juice of your choice (carrot, beetroot or spinach) into the flour and knead the coloured dough to a pliable texture. Cover and keep aside for 30 minutes. Roll out the coloured flour dough into a big thin rectangle. Form a ½ inch thick cylindrical shape with the plain dough and place in the middle of the coloured dough. Roll the coloured dough to cover the plain cylinder, cut away the excess dough. Pinch the edges of the coloured dough so no plain dough is visible to form a perfect long cylinder. Cut ½ inch thick round slices roll out into discs, the plain dough in the middle and the coloured dough at the edges, the wrapper for your rose *momo* is ready. Take three discs, overlap them with each other, place the filling in the middle, gently cover the filling, folding the lower disc over the top and pressing the edges. Roll gently from one side and fold over the other, making a perfect shape of a rose. Open out the petals a little and keep aside for 15 minutes. Steam for 20 minutes and serve hot.

A pretty way to serve this dish would be to make a leaf shape out of spinach juice *momos* and serve together.

Prawn/Fish Momo

*In Nepal, buari or catfish is suggested to make momos with,
because it has the minimum amount of bones.*

Preparation time: 30 minutes
Serves: 8-10, Makes: 50 momos

INGREDIENTS

½ kg minced prawn/catfish
1 cup chopped green onions
2 tbsp. finely chopped garlic
2 tbsp. light soya bean sauce
1 tbsp. lemon juice
1 tbsp. corn starch
1 tsp. chilli flakes
½ tsp. pepper powder
2 tbsp. oil
2 tbsp. water
Salt to taste

VARIATION

*Add ½ cup grated carrots, cabbage and
chopped bak choy/spinach to the minced
prawn /fish*

PREPARATION

Mix all the ingredients well, rest for 30 minutes. Roll
out thin discs and place 1 tsp. of filling in the middle of
the disc and make the shape of your choice. Since these
momos cook quickly, an open *momo* or *siu mai* looks very
attractive. Steam for 10 minutes and serve with the sauce
of your choice. *Siu mais* are usually served with four
sauces, one for each opening, creating an explosion of
different tastes in the mouth. The gentle flavour of prawn
or fish is lost to very strong sauces, so a light coriander
mint or chilli oil are suggested.

Momo Sizzler

Preparation time: 45 minutes
Serves: 1

INGREDIENTS

6 chicken/pork steamed momos
2 medium-sized cabbage leaves
1 cup mixed vegetables of your choice
½ cup grilled or pan-fried potatoes
1 medium-sized tomato
1 cup boiled noodles
1 cup gravy
1 tsp. oregano
1 tsp. coarsely ground pepper
Salt to taste

PREPARATION

Steam the *momos* of your choice from the previous recipes, like vegetarian, chicken, mutton or pork. *Kothes* or pan-fried *momos* are a good choice as well. Cut vegetables like carrots, zucchini, beans and cauliflower, boil for 3 minutes and keep aside. Pan-fry the potatoes till they are cooked and keep aside. Cut the top off the tomato and scoop out the pulp and stuff it with yak/ mozzarella cheese, pan-fry till the cheese melts and keep aside. Boil the cabbage leaves for 2 minutes and drain. Heat the sizzler pan till steaming hot, place the cabbage leaves on it, place the steamed/pan-fried *momos* on one side and the noodles on the other, decorate the vegetables, tomato and potatoes in the middle. Drizzle gravy or an *achar* of your choice on top of the *momos* and vegetables, sprinkle the seasoning on top, add 2 tsp. of butter under the cabbage leaf on the hot pan just before serving, this will make the pan sizzle and smoke. Serve sizzling hot!

Egg Pan-Fried Momo

Preparation time: 30 minutes
Serves: 4

INGREDIENTS

4 eggs
8 steamed momos of your choice
¼ tsp. onion seeds
1 tbsp. finely chopped green onions
2 tsp. oil
Salt to taste

PREPARATION

Beat the eggs in a bowl and add the salt to it and keep aside. Oil a frying pan and lay the *momos* in it, slowly pour the beaten egg into the pan, cover the pan and cook on low heat till the eggs are set and cooked. Garnish with the onion seeds and chopped green onions, cut in slices with a *momo* in the middle and serve with *achar* of your choice, preferably chilli oil.

Momo Chaat

Preparation time: 45 minutes
Serves: 2

INGREDIENTS

8 vegetarian/non-vegetarian momos of your choice
1 cup blended yogurt
½ cup tamarind chutney/sauce
½ cup coriander chutney/sauce
½ cup boiled and chopped potatoes
½ cup chopped onions
½ cup chopped tomatoes
½ cup boiled chickpeas
½ cup besan bhujuri (crunchy gram flour noodles)
2 tbsp. chopped coriander leaves
1 tsp. red chilli powder
2 tsp. chaat masala

PREPARATION

Prepare the *momos* of your choice according to the instructions in the recipe. I recommend the pan-fried or deep-fried ones. Drizzle the beaten yogurt, tamarind and coriander sauces over the *momos,* add the chickpeas, potatoes, chopped onions, tomatoes, *besan bhujuri,* garnish with chilli powder and *chaat masala* and chopped coriander. Serve immediately, otherwise the *momos* can get soggy.

Momo Choeyla

Chilli Momo

Chilli Momo

Preparation time: 30 minutes
Serves: 2

INGREDIENTS

10 steamed momos of your choice
1 tbsp. chopped garlic
2 tbsp. chopped green onions/onions
1 tsp. chopped green chillies
2 medium onions
2 medium capsicum
2 medium tomatoes
4 tbsp. oil
Salt to taste

CHILLI SAUCE
1 tbsp. hot chilli sauce
1 tbsp. soya sauce
2 ½ tbsp. sweet chilli garlic sauce
3 tbsp. ketchup

PREPARATION

Chop the onions, capsicum and tomatoes into quarters, keep aside. Use steamed, pan-fried or deep-fried *momos* according to your taste. Heat oil and sauté minced garlic, onion, and green chillies for 1 minute, add the chilli sauce mixture to the pan. Stir for 1 minute and add the vegetables and cook for 2 minutes. Add the *momos* and salt to taste, mix gently till all the ingredients are well coated with the chilli sauce.

Momo Choeyla

Spicy Tempered Momos

Preparation time: 30 minutes

Serves: 3

INGREDIENTS

12 momos of your choice
1 ½ tsp. ginger paste
1 tsp. garlic paste
½ tsp. timur powder
1 tsp. cumin powder
1 tsp. red chilli powder
½ cup chopped green garlic shoots
Salt to taste
1 tbsp. raw mustard oil
⅓ cup mustard oil
½ tsp. fenugreek seeds
½ tsp. turmeric powder

PREPARATION

Place the spices, ginger and garlic pastes, salt and 1 tbsp. raw mustard oil in a bowl. Mix till well integrated, add the *momos* and green garlic shoots, mix gently. Heat the ⅓ cup mustard oil in a pan and add the turmeric powder, swirl and pour over the *momos*. Serve hot or cold.

Khao Suey Momo

Momos in Burmese Soup

Khao suey is a Burmese soup made with noodles, chicken stock and coconut milk. It is garnished with various tasty toppings and is a very wholesome, delicious dish to have during a cold winter night. This fusion dish with an addition of momos is addictive.

Preparation time: 45 minutes
Serves: 4

INGREDIENTS

16 steamed or kothe momos
1 cup boiled noodles (optional)
¼ cup oil
1 tbsp. chopped garlic
½ cup chopped onions
1 tbsp. ginger paste
1 tbsp. garlic paste
½ cup chick pea flour
½ tsp. chilli powder
1 tbsp. coriander powder
½ tsp. turmeric powder
4 cups stock (vegetable/chicken/mutton/buff)
1 tbsp. fish sauce (optional)
1 tin coconut milk
Salt to taste

GARNISHING

1 cup chopped boiled eggs
1 cup chopped cooked bacon (optional)
1 cup chopped green onions
½ cup sliced onions
1 cup chopped coriander
1 cup fried garlic
1 cup fried noodles
3 lemons cut into wedges
½ cup bowl chilli flakes/chilli oil

PREPARATION

Steam the *momos* of your choice and keep aside.

KHAO SUEY SOUP

Heat the oil in a pan and add the chopped garlic and onions and stir till the onions are translucent. Add the ginger and garlic paste, stir for 1 minute. Add the chilli, turmeric and coriander powder and cook till the raw smell dissipates. Add the chickpea powder and cook till well integrated, now pour in the chicken stock and cook till the soup thickens a little, add the coconut milk and let soup come to a boil, add fish sauce and salt to taste. Pour the soup into the bowls, gently add the steamed *momos* into the soup and serve topped with the garnishing or allow the guests to garnish the soup according to their personal taste.

GARNISHING

Chop the eggs, bacon, shallots and coriander, deep-fry the chopped garlic, onions and noodles to a crispy golden colour, cut the lemons into wedges and place all the garnishing ingredients in separate bowls.

Chocolate Momo

Chocolate-Filled Momo

Preparation time: 30 minutes
Serves: 4

INGREDIENTS

2 cups grated brown/white chocolate
½ cup concentrated milk (kurani/khoya)
½ cup chopped nuts and raisins (optional)
Momo wrapper

GARNISHING
2 tbsp. chocolate sauce
2 tbsp. orange marmalade
1 tbsp. grated coconut

PREPARATION

Making larger *momos* for this dessert is ideal as the *momos* look nicer when served with different sauces as accompaniments. Grate the chocolate, mix with the concentrated milk and nuts. Roll out the wrapper into round discs and heap 2 tbsp. of the chocolate mix in the middle, press the filling into the wrapper and pinch the edges together in a pretty design. Steam the *momos* for 15 minutes, drizzle the chocolate sauce or marmalade on top of the *momos* and garnish with chopped nuts and grated coconut.

108

Golbheda Achar 1

Tomato Pickle 1

Preparation time: 30 minutes
Serves: 6

INGREDIENTS

6 chopped tomatoes
1 tbsp. mustard oil
½ tsp. fenugreek seeds
1 inch ginger
2 red chillies
2 tbsp. coriander leaves
Salt to taste

PREPARATION

Coarsely grind the red chillies and ginger. Heat oil in a pan, add the fenugreek seeds, cook till they turn black, add the chopped tomatoes, ginger and red chilli paste and salt, cook till it simmers and the tomatoes turn mushy. Add the chopped green coriander leaves and 2 cups of water and cook a further 5 minutes. This *achar* is of a thin, fluid consistency so add water if needed. Pour over the hot *momos*.

Til Ko Achar

Golbheda Achar

Dhaniya, Barbari Ko Achar

283

Golbheda Achar 2

Tomato Pickle 2

Preparation time: 30 minutes

Serves: 6

INGREDIENTS

6 tomatoes
3 big cloves garlic
1 medium onion
3 green chillies
½ inch piece ginger
½ tsp. timur powder
½ tsp. turmeric powder
1 tsp. red chilli powder
3 tbsp. sesame seed powder
3 tbsp. oil
Salt to taste

PREPARATION

Chop the vegetables roughly. Heat oil till it smokes, then add the garlic, onions, chillies, ginger and sauté for 1 minute. Add the sesame seeds and tomatoes and cook for 2 minutes, add the spices and cook till the tomatoes get mushy. Take off the fire and cool completely, blend to a smooth paste and serve with a dash of chilli oil.

Dhaniya, Barbari Ko Achar

Coriander, Mint Pickle

Preparation time: 15 minutes

Serves: 4

INGREDIENTS

1 cup coriander leaves
½ cup mint leaves
1 green chilli
1 garlic
2 tbsp. peanuts
½ lemon juice
Salt to taste

PREPARATION

Place all ingredients in a blender and mix to a nice smooth consistency, place in a bowl and serve with the *momos*.

Dhaniya, Haryo Pyaj Ko Achar

Coriander, Green Onion Pickle

Preparation time: 15 minutes
Serves: 6

INGREDIENTS

2 cups spring onions
1 cup chopped green coriander
2 tbsp. chopped garlic
1 tbsp. chopped ginger
½ cup sesame oil
¼ cup lemon juice
1 tbsp. finely chopped green chillies
Salt to taste

PREPARATION

Chop all the ingredients finely and mix together with the oil and lemon juice, add salt and serve.

Til Ko Achar

Sesame Seed Pickle

Preparation time: 15 minutes
Serves: 10

INGREDIENTS

1 cup sesame seeds
½ cup red chilli flakes
1 cup refined oil
Salt to taste

PREPARATION

Mix all the ingredients except the oil in a bowl, heat the oil and pour over the other ingredients, serve or preserve.

Nepali-English Terms

Aaloo	Potato	Dhindo	Porridge	Kur	Sherpa Flatbread	**R**akati	Blood Pudding
Achar	Pickle	Dodo	Wheat Flour Balls	Kwati	Sprouted Lentils	Rato Khursani	Red Chilli
Amilo	Sour	Dupka	Lentil Ball Soup	**I**skus	Chayote Squash	Ras	Soup
Anda	Egg	**G**aente Mula	Radish	**L**atte	Sticky Rice	Rayo	Mustard
Anadi	Sticky Rice			Lasun	Garlic	Rikikur	Sherpa Potato Pancake
Baaph	Steam	Gajar	Carrot	Ledo	Gravy	Rilduk	Sherpa Potato Soup
Bajaes	Brahmin Women	Gatani Daal	Horse Gram Lentil	Litti	Wheat Balls	Roth	Bread
Bakula	Broad Bean	Ghinti	Dried Blood Sausage	**M**aach	Fish	Roti	Bread
Bangur	Pig	Ghoongi	Snails	Maal Puwa	Rice Pancakes	**S**aag	Spinach
Bara	Lentil Pancakes	Ghyu	Ghee	Maas Daal	Split Black Gram	Sande Ko	Tempered
Barbari	Mint	Golbheda	Tomato	Macha	Fish	Sarson	Yellow Mustard Seeds
Baria	Lentil Cutlets	Gud	Molasses	Mada	Rice Flour Fried Crêpes		
Batuk	Lentil Doughnuts	Gundruk	Fermented Spinach	Maida	Refined Flour	Sekuwa	Barbecued
Bhaang	Hemp Seed			Makai	Corn	Shenlamu	Sautéed Liver
Bhaat	Cooked Rice	Gwaramari	Fried Flour Balls	Masala	Spice	Shyakpa	Sherpa Soup
Bhaddu	Brass Vessel	**H**aans	Duck	Masu	Meat	Shyaphale	Minced Meat Patties
Bhanti	Brinjal	Haryo	Green	Masuara	Dried Ground Lentil Ball		
Bhatmas	Dried Soya Beans	**J**eera	Cumin			Sukuti	Dried Meat
Bhatta	Dried Colocassia and Black Bean Soup	Jhaane Ko	Sautéed	Methi	Fenugreek	Surik	Pork
		Jhol	Stew	Mirch	Chilli	Sutkeri	Lactating
		Jhor	Curry	Mismas	Mixed	**T**aas	Spicy Mutton
Bhuja	Rice	Jimbu	Himalayan Allium	Momo	Steamed Dumplings	Tama	Fermented Bamboo
Biraula	Black-Eyed Beans	Jwano	Carom			Taral	Fried
Bodi	Black-Eyed Bean	**K**aalo	Black	Mula	Radish	Tare Ko	Fried
Buff	Buffalo	Kacho	Raw	Mungi	Petite Yellow Lentils	Tarkari	Vegetable
Chara	Chicken	Kadima	Pumpkin			Tarul	Yam
Chatamari	Rice Flour Pancake	Kakro	Cucumber	**N**anglo	Bamboo Mat	Taruwa	Deep-Fried
Chawal	Rice	Kalejo	Liver	Nesuse	Rice Flour Cake	Thekuwa	Biscuits
Cheura	Beaten Rice	Kanchemba	Buckwheat Fries	**P**akuwa	Cooked	Theeche ko	Crushed
Chimping	Nepali Hogweed	Katiya	Mutton Cooked in Earthen Pot	Palyo	Buttermilk	Thukpa	Sherpa Noodle Soup
Choeyla	Barbecue and Tempered			Parwal	Pointed Gourd		
		Kauli	Cauliflower	Phaphar	Buckwheat	Til	Sesame Seed
Chokha	Spiced	Kesara	Saffron	Pharsi	Pumpkin	Timur	Szechuan Pepper
Chope	Powdered Spices	Kerau	Peas	Phapchung	Butter Tea	Tingmo	Steamed Bun
Chukauni	Yogurt Salad	Khapse	Sherpa Biscuits	Philunge	Niger Seed	Titaura	Lentil Balls
Chaulani	Rice Starch Water	Khasi	Goat	Phing	Glass Noodles	Urad	Black Gram
Chuk Amilo	Concentrated Lemon Juice	Kheer	Rice Pudding	Phokso	Lungs	**W**o	Lentil Pancake
		Khursani	Chilli	Pla	Dried Meat, Potato Curry	**Y**omari	Steamed Rice Dumplings
Daal	Lentil	Kinema	Fermented Soya Bean				
Dahi	Yogurt			Pole Ko	Charcoal Grilled	Yangben	Wild Edible Lichen
Dhapu	Big	Koche	Filled	Pulao	Rice Preparation		
Dhania	Coriander	Koiralo	Ebony Buds	Puri	Fried Bread		
Dhikari	Steamed Rice Flour Dough	Kukhura	Chicken	Pyaj	Onion		

List of Recipes

SHERPA

1 Kur *(Sherpa Flat Bread)*
2 Rilduk *(Sherpa Potato Soup)*
3 Aaloo Phing *(Potato Curry with Glass Noodles)*
4 Shyakpa/Thukpa *(Sherpa Soup)*
5 Rikikur *(Potato Pancake)*
6 Shyaphale *(Deep-Fried Minced Meat Patties)*
7 Khapse *(Traditional Sherpa Biscuits)*
8 Phapchung *(Butter Tea)*

THAKALI

9 Kanchemba *(Buckwheat Fries)*
10 Phapar Ko Dhindo *(Buckwheat Porridge)*
11 Dodo *(Wheat Flour Balls with Spices)*
12 Bhatta *(Dried Colocasia and Black Soya Bean Soup)*
13 Ghinti *(Dried Blood Sausage)*
14 Pla *(Potato, Bean and Sukuti/Dried Meat Curry)*
15 Ngyoshol *(Wild Goosefoot Spinach and Yogurt)*
16 Mula Theeche Ko Achar *(Crushed Radish Fresh Pickle)*
17 Timur Chope *(Sichuan Pickle)*
18 Mustang Aaloo *(Mustang Potatoes)*
19 Sukuti Hale Ko Kaalo Bodi Daal *(Mustang Daal with Dried Yak Meat)*

THAKURI/BAHUN/CHETRI/KHAS

20 Dupka *(Lentil Ball Soup)*
    Gatani Daal Ko Dupka/Palyo *(Horse Gram Lentils Cooked in Buttermilk)*
21 Chaulani *(Tempered Lentil Balls in Rice Starch Water)*
22 Bhaddu Ma Pakai Ko Khasi Pakuwa *(Mutton Cooked in a Brass Vessel)*
23 Dahi Hale Ko Macha *(Fish Cooked in Yogurt Sauce)*
24 Maas Daal Roth *(Bread Stuffed with Black Gram)*
25 Mada *(Rice Flour Crêpes)*
26 Koiralo Ko Achar *(Ebony Buds Fresh Pickle)*
27 Nesuse *(Rice Flour Cake)*
28 Khasi Masu Gaente Mula Ko Ledo *(Radish and Mutton Curry)*
29 Khasi Masu Kauli Kerau *(Mutton Cooked with Cauliflower and Peas)*
30 Kwati Chara Tare Ko *(Fried Mixed Sprouted Beans and Chicken)*

31 Masu Koche Ko Parwal *(Pointed Gourd Stuffed with Minced Chicken)*
32 Aaloo Chukauni *(Potatoes and Yogurt Salad)*
    Aaloo Pyaj Ko Ras *(Potatoes and Onion Soup)*
    Aaloo Bakula *(Potatoes and Broad Beans)*
    Aaloo Chuk *(Potatoes with Concentrated Lemon Juice)*
33 Paani Roti *(Wheat Bread in Lentil Soup)*
34 Iskus Tare Ko *(Fried Chayote Squash)*
35 Raayo Saag *(Mustard Greens)*
36 Bhaang Ko Achar *(Hemp Seed Pickle)*
37 Aaloo Gajar Kerau Ko Achar *(Potato, Carrot and Fresh Peas Pickle)*
38 Haryo Lasun Sande Ko *(Tempered Green Garlic Shoots)*
    Haryo Lasun Dahi Hale Ko *(Green Garlic Shoots in Yogurt)*
39 Makai Ko Kheer *(Fresh Corn Pudding)*
40 Gud Bhuja *(Rice with Molasses)*

TAMANG

41 Buff Sukuti Ko Ledo *(Dried Buffalo Meat Gravy)*
42 Batuk *(Fried Black Lentil Doughnuts)*
43 Phapar Ko Phulaura *(Buckwheat Fluffy Balls)*

MAGAR

44 Makai Ko Dhindo *(Maize Porridge)*
45 Tarul Tare Ko *(Fried Yam)*
46 Sutkeri Kukhura Ko Jhol *(Local Chicken Curry for Nursing Mothers)*

GURUNG

47 Latte *(Sweet Sticky Rice)*
48 Kukhura Ko Masu Ko Achar *(Chicken Pickle)*
49 Bodi Ko Biraula *(Black-Eyed Beans)*
50 Gundruk Aaloo Bodi Tare Ko *(Fried Fermented Dried Greens, Potatoes and Soya Beans)*

NEWAR

51 Wo Bara *(Green Gram Lentil Pancakes)*
    Maas Daal Ko Bara *(Deep-Fried Black Gram Lentil Pancakes)*
52 Chatamari *(Rice Pancake with Minced Meat and Egg)*
53 Haans Ko Choeyla *(Barbecued Tempered Duck Meat)*
54 Phokso Tare Ko *(Batter Fried Lung)*
55 Shenlamu *(Sautéed Liver)*
56 Parwal Tare Ko *(Fried Pointed Gourd)*
57 Kauli Tarkari *(Tempered Cauliflower)*
58 Saag Sande Ko *(Tempered Spinach)*
59 Yomari *(Steamed Rice Dumplings Filled with Molasses)*
60 Gwamari *(Deep-Fried Flour Balls)*

RAI AND LIMBU

61   Kaalo Bangur Ko Masu, Bhatmas Ra Rayo *(Pork with Soya Beans and Mustard Greens)*
62   Yangben *(Wild Edible Lichen)*
63   Tarkari Haleko Yangben *(Yangben with Vegetables)*
64   Kinema *(Fermented Soya Beans)*
65   Chimping, Golbheda Ko Achar *(Nepali Hogweed and Tomato Achar)*
66   Philunge Ko Achar *(Jhuse Til/Niger Seed Powder Pickle)*

THARU

67   Dhikari *(Steamed Rice Flour Dough in Different Shapes)*
68   Baria *(Deep-Fried Lentil Cutlets)*
69   Anadi Chawal Ko Roti *(Sweet Deep-Fried Rice Flour Bread)*
70   Ghoongi *(Snails Curry)*
71   Surik Sekuwa *(Charcoal Grilled Pork)*
72   Sidra Macchi *(Deep-Fried and Tempered Small Fish)*
73   Tharu Aaloo *(Tharu Tempered Potatoes)*
74   Bair Chutney *(Wild Indian Plum Chutney)*

MADESH

75   Taas Ko Masu *(Spicy Dry Mutton)*
76   Mula Ko Achar *(Radish Pickle)*
77   Katiya Masu *(Mutton Cooked in an Earthen Pot)*
78   Chawal Ko Roti *(Rice Flour Bread)*
79   Tarkari Ko Achar *(Mixed Vegetable Pickle)*
80   Aaloo Chokha *(Spiced Potatoes)*
81   Litti *(Wheat Balls Stuffed with Spiced Lentils)*
82   Thekuwa *(Sweet Biscuits)*
83   Maal Puwa *(Crispy Fried Pancakes)*

MITHILA

84   Machha Ke Jhor *(Fish Curry)*
85   Taral Maach *(Fried Fish)*
86   Taruwa *(Deep-Fried Vegetables Coated in Rice Flour)*
87   Kadima *(Sautéed Pumpkin and Peas)*
88   Bhanti *(Sautéed Eggplants)*

MOMOS

89 Vegetable Momo
90 Momocha *(Newari Momo)*
91 Chicken Momo
92 Mutton/Pork Momo
93 Jhol Momo *(Momos Served in a Soup)*
94 Chara/Khasi/Buff Ko Ras *(Chicken/Mutton/Buff Soup)*
95 Kwati Ko Jhol Momo *(Momos in Sprouted Bean Soup)*
96 Tingmo *(Steamed Bun)*
97 Shogo Shabril Momo *(Tibetan Potato Meat Momos)*
98 Dhapu Momo *(Giant Momo)*

FUSION MOMOS

99 Rose Momo
100 Prawn/Fish Momo
101 Momo Sizzler
102 Egg Pan-Fried Momo
103 Momo Chaat
104 Chilli Momo
105 Momo Choeyla *(Spicy Tempered Momos)*
106 Khao Suey Momo *(Momos in Burmese Soup)*
107 Chocolate Momo *(Chocolate-Filled Momo)*
108 Golbheda Achar 1 *(Tomato Pickle 1)*
    Golbheda Achar 2 *(Tomato Pickle 2)*
    Dhaniya, Barbari Ko Achar *(Coriander, Mint Pickle)*
    Dhaniya, Haryo Pyaj Ko Achar *(Coriander, Green Onion Pickle)*
    Til Ko Achar *(Sesame Seed Pickle)*

Acknowledgements

I am forever grateful to my mother,
Rajamata Anant Kumari of Awagarh,
for teaching me humility, compassion, living graciously and initiating me to culinary delights.

My father and mother-in-law
Hon. ADC General to HM King Birendra Bikram Shah Deva,
Maj. Gen. Aditya S.J.B. Rana and Rani Sunita Rana,
for their love and trust.

My brother and sister-in-law
Raja Anirudha Pal Singh and Rani Anjali Kumari,
for their unconditional love and support.

My husband's Didi (nanny) Chiniya Champa, who taught me everything I know about Nepali cooking.
I am most grateful to my friends and family for giving me their
precious time, recipes, lending me their crockery, jewellery and fabric,
regaling me with anecdotes and making this book possible.

I thoroughly enjoyed working with the talented Mannsi Agrawal, my photographer,
to whom I owe most of the beautiful food images in this book.

The Image Ark team,
Marie Ange Holmgren-Sylvain, a highly talented team leader, for your discerning eye.
Swojan Newa, for your tireless effort and meticulous professionalism.
Mrigaja Bajracharya, for your stunning artwork.
Thank you for proofreading and artistically designing this book for me.

Keshav Raj Bhattrai, for tirelessly trying out and documenting recipes with me.
Thanks to Sunil Nakarmi, my computer specialist.

Last but definitely not least, my publishers, Penguin Random House India,
for placing their trust in me again and bringing this book to fruition.
Thank you, Milee Ashwarya, Manasi Subramaniam and Archana Nathan,
for your continued support.

Special Thanks To
(in alphabetical order)

A special thanks to all for helping me in my research on the various ethnic communities, providing me with recipes, jewellery and costumes that I have included in this book. Your invaluable inputs and help have led to the creation of this book.

Mrs Mangala Amatya

Mr Yogeshwar Amatya

Mrs Merina Bajracharya

Mrs Sankata Chaudhary

Mr Sitaram Chaudhary

Mrs Punita Chaudhary

Mrs Kamala Gurung

NCE Rasham Gurung

Mrs Sangita Tangbetani Gurung

Ms Bhawana Karki

Mrs Sarita Karki

Lt Col Ravi Jung Khadka

Ms Sita Lama

Mrs Indu Limbu

Mrs Alka Pathak

Mrs Alka Rana

Mrs Brinda Rana

Mrs Laxmi Rana

Dr Niti Rana

Mrs Rama Rana

Mrs Sheila Rana

Mrs Sharda Rana

Mrs Ujjawala Rana

Mrs Shaguni Singh Sakya

Mr Janakraj Sapkota

Mrs Netra Rajya Laxmi Shah

Mrs Laxmi Shakya

Mr Ang Dawa Sherpa

Mrs Sabita Shrestha

Mrs Susan Shrestha

Mrs Rashmi Shrivastav

Mrs Rumi Shrivastav

Mrs Rita Simha

Mrs Ingwa Subba

Mr Dev Tamrakar

Sgt Bikas Thapa

Mrs Pratima Thapa

Mrs Sangita Thapa

Mrs Kamal Tuladhar

Mr Vivek Upadhyaya

Scan QR code to access the
Penguin Random House India website